Daniel Gawthrop

D0782843

VANISHING
HALO

SAVING THE BOREAL FOREST

David Suzuki Foundation

GREYSTONE BOOKS
DOUGLAS & McINTYRE PUBLISHING GROUP
VANCOUVER/TORONTO

THE
MOUNTAINEERS
SEATTLE

Greystone Books
A division of Douglas & McIntyre Ltd.
2323 Quebec Street, Suite 201
Vancouver, British Columbia   V5T 4S7

Published by
The Mountaineers
1001 SW Klickitat Way, Suite 201
Seattle, Washington   98134

David Suzuki Foundation
2211 West 4th Avenue, Suite 219
Vancouver, British Columbia   V6K 4S2

Canadian Cataloguing in Publication Data

Gawthrop, Daniel, 1963–
  Vanishing halo

  Includes bibliographical references and index.
  ISBN 1-55054-729-1

  1. Taigas. 2. Taiga ecology. I. Title.
QH541.5.T3G39 1999   577´.37   C99-910819-0

Library of Congress Cataloging-in-Publication data
A catalog record for this book is available at the Library of Congress.
ISBN 0-89886-681-2

Editing by Nancy Flight
Cover design by Peter Cocking
Typesetting by Brenda and Neil West, BN Typographics West
Map by Stuart Daniel
Printed and bound in Canada by Friesens

The publishers gratefully acknowledge the assistance of the Canada Council and of the British Columbia Ministry of Tourism, Small Business and Culture. The publisher also acknowledges the financial support of the Government of Canada through the Book Publishing Industry Development Program.
Canadä

The books in the David Suzuki Foundation Series explore issues of crucial environmental significance, with an emphasis on finding solutions.

The publishers gratefully acknowledge the contribution of Friesens in providing paper for this book that is 50 per cent recycled and 20 per cent post-consumer waste.

Contents

Foreword

The David Suzuki Foundation was established in 1990 to find concrete ways of achieving a sustainable balance between humankind's social, economic, and ecological needs. We communicate our findings to all levels of society and develop strategies for change with local grassroots individuals and groups, for we believe that change does not trickle down from the top but rises from local communities to government and corporate levels. We also believe that there is still time to change the way we live and to create a brighter future.

We are impelled by the sense of urgency in the Warning to Humanity signed by 1600 senior scientists from seventy-one countries and over half of all living Nobel Prize winners: "Human beings and the natural world are on a collision course ... many of our current practices put at serious risk the future that we wish ... and may so alter the world that it will be unable to sustain life in the manner that we know ... No more than one or a few decades remain before the chance to avert the threats we now confront will be lost." (The Union of Concerned Scientists, November 1992)

For decades, alarming signs of environmental degradation across the planet have been reported. Now overpopulation, toxic pollution, atmospheric change, deforestation, soil degradation, and so on are directly affecting people's lives. In addition, it has become clear that the economy and social issues are inextricably intertwined with the environment.

In a mere century, humanity has been transformed into a super-species able to change the very biological and physical make-up of the Earth. Our scientific and technological prowess has allowed us to increase our consumption of energy and resources, produce pollutants, and destroy ecosystems. At the same time, our shift from the countryside to the city has broken our contact with nature and freed the global economy to push for endless growth, ransacking our children's future.

As biological beings, we depend on the quality of the air, water, and soil and on the biodiversity of life on Earth for our survival. The David Suzuki Foundation aims to document the perilous state of our ecological life-support systems while identifying those nations, regions, groups, or individuals who are working to achieve sustainable living. The good news is that most experts believe that a sustainable future is possible and that there is still time to bring it about.

The David Suzuki Foundation Series is part of the communication of our work. We hope that the books in this series will illuminate both the challenges that face us and the possibilities for a sustainable future for us all.

David Suzuki
Chair, David Suzuki Foundation

Preface

In fall 1971, when I was eight years old and growing up on Vancouver Island in British Columbia, I heard an announcement on TV that the U.S. Department of Defense—ignoring all advice to the contrary—had decided to conduct a third underground nuclear test at Amchitka, the westernmost bead of the Aleutians, a string of islands that connect North America to the Russian Far East. The first nuclear blast, called Long Shot, was an 80-kilotonne explosion that contaminated the atmosphere with radioactive pollution. The second, known as Milrow, caused similar radioactive contamination and triggered a massive rockslide on the Bering coast. Now, the Atomic Energy Commission was planning a 5-megatonne blast at Cannikin that would cost more than U.S.$200 million. It was to be the largest, most expensive underground nuclear test ever.

Despite an international campaign that crossed ideological boundaries, editorials by the *Washington Post* and *New York Times*, and an urgent plea by five federal agencies opposed to the test, American president Richard Nixon pushed ahead.

Too young to appreciate Amchitka's political nuances, I was more fascinated by its science. In the final days before the blast, this warning from an Alaskan seismologist captured my imagination:

> This station not only recorded the Milrow event, but also detected an alarming influx of earthquakes directly following the test ... Further testing by the AEC [Atomic Energy Commission] could trigger more earthquakes, not only in Alaska, and no one can predict what disastrous results may be forthcoming.

I knew that the 1964 Anchorage earthquake had caused a tidal wave that traveled down the Pacific coast, even rolling up Alberni Inlet just an hour or two along the Vancouver Island Highway from my home town. I also had vivid memories of Margaret Hodges's *The Wave* (which I read in grade two), a classic children's story about a Japanese fishing village whose four hundred inhabitants—facing imminent death from a tsunami—are offered last-minute salvation by the wise man on the hill. Those memories, combined with Cold War nuclear phobia, gave me sleepless nights.

Of course, no such tidal wave crashed upon Vancouver Island following the Cannikin blast of November 6, 1971. Later, friends would scoff at my fear that the test could possibly affect us. We were, after all, safely cocooned in a temperate southern suburb nestled along the 49th parallel. But the memory of Amchitka remained with me forever, for two reasons.

First, a nuclear explosion of such magnitude offered dramatic evidence of the havoc that human activity can wreak on the natural world. The Cannikin blast registered 7.0 on the Richter scale. It blew open an 18-meter (60-foot) crater more than 1.6 kilometers (1 mile) wide, triggered massive rockslides, and released huge clouds of radioactive gas into the atmosphere, instantly killing thousands of ducks, several hundred sea otters, and untold numbers of fish, birds, and other marine mammals that the Aleut First Nations people depended on for survival.

Second, the media's focus on a remote Alaskan island provided a sobering glimpse into the mysterious world of the North. Until those Greenpeace activists set sail on the *Phyllis Cormack* in a failed bid to stop the test, the "frozen North" had never existed as a real place in my consciousness. It was "out there"—a mythical, clichéd landscape of glaciers and snow where the tundra began and civilization ended. Nothing that occurred in the North seemed to matter, because what happened there surely could not affect life elsewhere.

But Amchitka opened my eyes. I realized that people living near the Cannikin blast may have been exposed to radiation and that many forms of animal life traveled the North's landscape, just as many fish species swam in its waters. And if those fish ever swam near "temperate zone" fish, I reasoned, some of those fish would eventually swim near the fish of Departure Bay—where I lived—and perhaps contaminate my food source. Simplistic logic? Perhaps. But environmental impact studies over the following three decades would repeatedly tell us that all ecosystems are interdependent, that the actions of human beings in one ecosystem affect other ecosystems, and that much of the damage we do to the planet is irreversible.

Nearly three decades after that final Amchitka blast, the Cold War rhetoric having long since faded from newspaper headlines, the planet's North faces another disaster. This danger is less apocalyptic than Amchitka, its politics more subtle, and its effects harder to predict than the aftermath of a nuclear explosion. But its consequences will probably affect a greater number of people. For the last hundred years, the great boreal forest—a coniferous green halo that is one-third of the world's forest cover—has been disappearing. Global warming—which has increased the number

of forest fires in the boreal region—has, together with unregulated clear-cut logging and other industrial activities, depleted
the world's boreal ecosystem. As *Vanishing Halo* reveals, the loss
of the boreal forest could have serious consequences for more
than the million or so people living there. Such a loss will affect
the atmosphere, the water supply, and the transportation routes—
to say nothing of the timber source—of many millions of people
living in the temperate zone below the boreal belt.

By writing this book, I hope to help make more residents of
the temperate south aware of the incredible boreal ecosystem and
its importance to the balance of the global environment. After
learning about the boreal forest's rich biodiversity, its unique aboriginal cultures, and its basic ecology, perhaps more people will
question their governments the next time a license is approved for
industrial activity in an old-growth boreal forest. After learning
about some of the solutions developed for the region, perhaps
more people will be inspired to apply those same or similar solutions elsewhere. If nothing else, I hope *Vanishing Halo* will provide some much-needed publicity for an ecosystem that has long
been neglected in favor of its more exotic cousins, the temperate
and tropical rain forests. As the final frontier for transnational
timber, petroleum, and mining interests, the great boreal forest
needs some long overdue attention.

Acknowledgments

My involvement with this book began in spring 1998 when Canadian writer and philosopher Stan Persky encouraged me to submit a proposal to the David Suzuki Foundation and Greystone Books. I was by no means a forest expert and had little knowledge of the boreal ecosystem. But with Stan's gentle persuasion, I was convinced of the subject's importance and endeavored to write a book that would appeal to a broad audience.

I am grateful to many people for their help. For a crash course on boreal culture, biodiversity, and industrial hot spots, I'm especially indebted to the Taiga Rescue Network. At the fourth Taiga Rescue Network conference, held in Tartu, Estonia, in October 1998, several participants provided interviews or ideas: Otso Ovaskainen, Virpi Sahi, Andrei Laletin, Josh Newell, Anatoly Lebedev, Jan von Boeckel, Natalia Cherbakova, Olga Galchinova, Mary Rees, Stephanie Hitztaler, Jutta Kill, Julia Siniakova, Jonas Rudberg, Jarmo Pyyko, Knut-Erik Helle, Mikhail Karpachevskiy, Dmitri Aksenov, Jan Henriksson, Urpo Taskinen, Daniel Thorell and Pernilla Hansson, Harald Helander, Elissa Peter, David

Whyte, Kaisa Raitio, Matti Liimatainen, Charles Restino, and Colleen McCrory.

Another of my Canadian contacts at the conference, Don Sullivan of Manitoba's Future Forest Alliance, flew me to his home province to visit a southern boreal forest community and meet Garry and Raymond Raven, and an Anishanaabe elder Fabian Morriseau, who provided insight into the effect of industrial development on traditional ways of life.

I'm also grateful to James Allen of the Champagne-Aishihik First Nations in Yukon for his comments on comanagement and traditional environmental knowledge; Werner Kurz, Stewart Cohen, and Glenn Juday, for their perspectives on climate change; and especially Mike Robinson at the Arctic Institute of North America, who provided a comprehensive overview of the politics and anthropology of traditional environmental knowledge and co-management regimes. David Hocking, Dermot Foley, and others from the David Suzuki Foundation read the manuscript and offered helpful suggestions, as did forest ecologist Stan Rowe and journalist Ben Parfitt. I'm especially grateful to Ben for his sustained interest in the project, and to Tom Sandborn and Terry Glavin, for their much-needed advice and support during its most difficult phase.

Warren O'Briain provided a Salt Spring Island retreat; my father, Paul Gawthrop, the use of his Nanaimo home; Evan Adams, a Calgary crashpad; and Bernard von Schulmann, his usual wisdom on ecopolitics. Don Larventz reviewed the outline and early parts of the manuscript, and kept my spirits up.

The biggest thanks, however, go to my editor at Greystone, Nancy Flight, whose calm professionalism and good humour arrived at just the right point in the project to guarantee its completion. Without her, you wouldn't be holding this book.

Prologue

April 12, 1961

Fourteen minutes after blasting off from a top secret Soviet launchpad, the spacecraft *Vostok* reached an altitude of 300 kilometers (200 miles) and separated from its canopy, sending the 27-year-old pilot into orbit. Strapped snugly inside the capsule, Yuri Gagarin took humankind's first glimpse of the planet Earth from outer space.

A stunning view of the Northern Hemisphere greeted him. Ringing the circumpolar north was a giant green halo—a vast expanse of coniferous forest stretching across the subarctic latitudes of Russia, Scandinavia, and North America. This area was the boreal forest, the world's largest forest ecosystem, encompassing one-third of the planet's forest cover—much of it spread across the young cosmonaut's native Russia. Gagarin viewed many other parts of the earth during his historic flight, but as *Vostok* circled the globe, orbiting the earth in one hour and forty-eight minutes, the sight of this giant green halo must have been overwhelming.

What Gagarin didn't realize as he completed his flight, eject-
ing from the *Vostok* at 7000 meters (23,000 feet) and parachuting
to safety in Siberia, was that the boreal forest was already disappearing. By the time American astronauts were joining their
Russian counterparts on the space station Mir nearly four
decades later, Gagarin's once-majestic view of unbroken boreal
forest was withering into a sad patchwork of managed second-
growth forests and burned woodlands dotted with clear-cuts and
geological seismic lines. At the northern margins, the coniferous
treeline was squeezing into the tundra; in the south, hardwood
forests were gradually converting to grassland. The green halo
was vanishing.

CHAPTER I

A Walk
in the Woods

There are some who can live without wild things, and some who
cannot ... For those of us in the minority, the opportunity to see
geese is more important than television.

—Aldo Leopold, quoted in *A Sand County Almanac*

Jarvselja, Estonia
October 8, 1998

On a glorious fall day in southeastern Estonia, I am wandering
along a lonely trail deep within a sub-boreal forest of birch, pine,
and spruce. It's about 8°C (46°F), and the air is crisp and clean.
The sun—shining brightly in an endless blue sky—casts a golden
light as it filters through the leaves of birch that line this path for
miles. A gentle breeze sweeps down the trail, caressing the leaves
like waves on a beach. For a moment, I forget that I'm thousands
of miles from home, in a former Soviet republic whose language
and culture I can't begin to comprehend.

I am on a field trip as part of an international conference on
boreal forests organized by the Taiga Rescue Network, a global
working group of nongovernmental organizations (NGOS) that
have tried, since the network was formed in 1992, to preserve the
world's boreal forests. Among the 150 ecologists and NGO activists
from Scandinavia, Eurasia, and North America who began the
conference two days ago, I'm the only journalist.

The 6000-hectare (15,000-acre) lot we're visiting is known in Estonia as a *peravald*, or managed backwoods—part of a study and research center for forestry students. About a two hours' drive south of Tartu, the university town where the conference began, it's a mixed forest of primeval and second-growth tree stands. The boreal species here are dominated by hardwoods such as birch and alder, but the area we're walking through is largely coniferous.

At the *peravald*, we've seen everything from bog forests to the remains of old timber rafting canals, used by foresters earlier in the 20th century to drag cut trees from the forest, including some of the highest trees in Estonia. Taking a deep breath, we smell the rich, moist fragrance of fresh soil and peat bogs. There are drainage ditches everywhere—artificial barriers, we're told, to level the uneven tilting of ground that caused the water to flow south and create marshlike conditions. The woods are filled with soil-dwelling fungi. Later, turning onto another trail, I meet a few other delegates, who convince me to eat some red huckleberries. I hesitate at first, recalling a berry of similar color that gave me a stomachache as a child. But these tangy berries are perfectly edible. So far, the botany lesson is going well: on my first visit north of the temperate zone in a land thousands of miles from Vancouver, where I live, I feel oddly at home in this forest.

Circling the Halo

Before taking this trip, I knew little about the boreal forest. Like many residents of the temperate south, I had no idea that it forms the largest forest ecosystem and one of the last frontier landscapes in the world. I didn't even know why it was called the boreal forest.

Taken from the Latin *Boreas,* god of the north wind, the word "boreal" is a catchall term for things northern. *Aurora borealis* is Latin for northern lights, those remarkable lights that can be seen in the night sky throughout much of the Arctic. Boreal forests, or northern forests, are frequently referred to as the *taiga*, a Russian word that originally signified a "dense marshy forest in Siberia" but is now used for all boreal and coniferous forests in the Northern Hemisphere.

The boreal forest forms the longest natural border in the world, a continuous belt of green broken only by the Bering Sea and the northern Atlantic Ocean. This green halo dominates any map of the globe with the North Pole at its center.

The magnificent Russian taiga contains the largest unbroken tracts of forest in the world. Stretching from the Ural Mountains to the Pacific Ocean, these Russian woods include 54 percent of the world's coniferous forest and 21 percent of the planet's total forest area. At 4 million square kilometers (1.5 million square miles), that's nearly twice as large as Brazil's rain forest. Most of the Russian taiga lies in central and western Siberia.

*The magnificent Russian taiga contains the largest
unbroken tracts of forest in the world.*

One of the largest expanses of Siberian taiga lies in the northeastern republic of Sakha, also known by its traditional name of Yakutia. This republic covers one-fifth of the Russian Federation—an area comparable in size to India. It has more than 700,000 rivers, whose total length is about 1.5 million kilometers (900,000 miles). With 40 percent of its territory within the Arctic circle, it's also one of the coldest populated areas on the planet; winter temperatures may fall as low as -68°c (-90°F). Yakutia, which hosts one of the world's three boreal-region international centers for plant diversity, is known for its distinctive pine-strip forests: long, narrow, parallel bands of pine and aspen that grow for hundreds of kilometers along ancient riverbeds created from glacial runoff at the end of the last ice age.

The boreal forest forms the longest natural border in the world, a coniferous belt of green broken only by the Bering Sea and the northern Atlantic Ocean. *Adapted from the Boreal Forest map, published by* Canadian Geographic *and Environment Canada.*

In October 1995, Russian president Boris Yeltsin issued a decree stating that up to 50 percent of the Russian Arctic should be placed under strict governmental protection. In response, the government of Yakutia pledged to extend the republic's system of protected areas to 700,000 square kilometers (270,000 square miles) of virgin territory—an area roughly twice the size of Germany—by the year 2000.

European Russia has two significant belts of boreal old-growth: the Komi Republic forest along the Ural Mountains, and the Green Belt of Karelia, along the Russian-Finnish border. The Komi Republic contains 2.5 million hectares (6 million acres) of pristine boreal forest. The Green Belt of Karelia is one of Europe's three remaining old-growth forest frontiers. According to Russian environmentalists, only 10 to 15 percent of the region's old-growth forests were still standing in 1996. Even that small percentage is under threat because of the forest's importance to the Karelian economy: resource-poor apart from its forests, Karelia derives 60 percent of its local revenues from the forest industry.

Most of the Scandinavian forest is boreal, dominated by Scots pine and Norway spruce; it also contains birch trees. In Finland, 66 percent of the total land base is productive forest land; 57 percent of Sweden and 23 percent of Norway can be described as productive forest land. The north of Sweden is home to what has been called "the largest remaining functioning boreal forest ecosystem in western Europe." The Njakafjall forest area covers 2600 hectares (6400 acres) in the north of Sweden close to the Norwegian border. That's about all that's left of the old-growth forests that once covered most of Sweden. Less than 3 percent of productive forest land in the country is protected in nature reserves or national parks.

After the Russian taiga, the world's largest expanse of frontier forest lies in North America—an unbroken 6500-kilometer (4000-mile) arc of boreal forest stretching from Newfoundland on the east coast all the way across the continent, covering more than half of the Prairie provinces, all of Yukon, and most of Alaska. According to a 1997 report of the World Resources Institute, 25 percent of the world's remaining frontier forests lie in Canada's boreal region. The boreal ecosystem is the largest type of forest in Canada, covering 341 million hectares (843 million acres)—of which about 180 million hectares (445 million acres) is considered harvestable for commercial purposes.

At the end of the boreal belt, America's northernmost state of Alaska is filled with white spruce on the river flood plains and black spruce and lodgepole pine in the uplands. Owned mostly by the state and private Native corporations, boreal forests make up 90 percent of the forest cover in Alaska, with more than 46 million hectares (113.6 million acres) of boreal trees. The largest of these regions is the Tanana Basin watershed, which covers 8.5 million hectares (21 million acres).

INSIDE THE TAIGA

> *The lake was as still as I'd ever seen it ... Swainson's thrush songs mingled with those of hermit thrushes, along with the occasional song of the Lincoln's sparrow. Four silver-haired bats flapped slowly across the water's surface, once even at eye level between myself and the bow of the canoe. Cupping my hands to my ears I could hear the repetitive notes of the saw-whet owl. Then a lone barred owl boomed its eight distinctive notes and did so again three or four more times ... As I returned to the shore, fireflies twinkled like fairies and from the darkness a white-throated sparrow sang "Oh dear, sweet Canada, Canada, Canada."*

> —University of Alberta conservationist Jim Butler,
> describing a trip to the Lakeland region
> (*Western Canada Wilderness Committee Report*, spring 1996)

In the north, the boreal forest extends to the tundra. In the south, it is bounded by the southern temperate forests. The real boreal forest begins in a transition zone, or ecotone, where cold-tolerant conifers (pine, spruce, fir, tamarack) generally replace cold-sensitive hardwoods (birch, poplar, willow, alder, aspen) as the major tree species. In this zone, hardwoods are a minor presence.

Until twenty years ago or so, boreal ecologists argued about the exact boundaries separating the boreal forest from the southern temperate forests. Some tried to use 60 degrees latitude as a kind of generic borderline. Today, however, a quick scan of any weather map reveals that the boreal landscape is determined more by complex climate patterns than by strict latitudinal boundaries. In North America, for example, the boreal region falls well below 60 degrees—covering most of Ontario and Quebec. This boundary puts the boreal forest much closer to civilization than many of us realize: Ottawa is only a two-hour drive from its edge. Quebec City, Winnipeg, and Edmonton are even closer. In Eurasia, the taiga falls south of Russia into northern China and Mongolia.

The boreal ecosystem is a complex, interconnected web of shrubs, trees, herbs, mosses, lichens, microorganisms, insects, and animals. These organisms are essentially the same throughout the boreal forest. Similar species of spruce, pine, and birch can be found in Thunder Bay, Ontario, and in the forests of Finland. Similar shrub and herb species—such as the twinflower, the bog cranberry, and the bearberry—are present in both the North American and the Eurasian boreal zones. The same could be said for animal species.

Some members of the forest industry have referred to the boreal forests, rather unfortunately, as a "species-poor" ecosystem. This term may be a more accurate reflection of the number and size of individual trees rather than the number of species within the forest. Boreal trees do not usually reach the towering heights, or grow in the same dense clusters, as those of the temperate rain forests. Because of the cold climate, they tend to grow more slowly than in the temperate zone. In the north, hardy tamarack and black spruce hug the ground and grow so slowly as to be finger sized after a hundred years. In addition, large peat bogs separate the tree stands. As a result, the boreal forest—especially at the northern margins—looks something like open parkland: widely spaced trees, with open areas in between. Instead of calling it a forest, some ecologists prefer to use the term "boreal woodland."

The boreal landscape is determined more by complex climate patterns than by strict latitudinal boundaries.

Boreal tree species are well adapted to harsh northern climates where the growing season is short and soil is shallow and sparse. Conifers such as black spruce and balsam fir grow roots in the wet acidic soils of boreal peatlands. Others can grow on a shallow bed of soil over bare Precambrian rock. Because trees must constantly adapt to harsh conditions, genetic diversity is quite high in the boreal region, even though species diversity is relatively low.

Trees such as white birch, trembling aspen, balsam poplar, jack pine, white spruce, and tamarack can grow in either pure or mixed stands in a variety of conditions throughout the boreal region. Some species, such as pine and spruce, are more commonly found in even-aged stands created by fire; others, such as aspen and poplar, are more common in the prairie-forest transition zone, where soil is fresher and better drained.

One of the boreal forest's most dominant features is its vast peatland territory. Peat is a dense accumulation of water-saturated, partially decayed vegetable tissue. When it's dry, peat can be used as a fuel. (It is often the first stage in the formation of coal.) A traditional source of fuel in countries such as Ireland and Russia, peat is also dug into the soil to increase its capacity to retain moisture and serves as a source of plant food.

Peatlands are divided into two categories: bogs (areas of ground saturated with water and decayed vegetation) and fens (a lower, marshier type of land that is only partially covered with water if not drained). In the boreal forest, peatlands are an ecosystem unto themselves—nearly one-fifth of the boreal region is covered by deep layers of nondecomposing peat moss.

Since the end of the ice age, when the first plants sprouted from the fresh, new landscape, peat mounds have accumulated in bogs, lake bottoms, and depressions. These peat deposits serve as giant sponges, holding and releasing water in a constant flow. They are also giant carbon sinks, the largest source of carbon in the boreal forest. Thanks in large part to these vast peatlands, the boreal forest is the largest terrestrial storehouse of carbon on the planet and thus plays a key role in maintaining the earth's balance of oxygen and carbon dioxide.

Here's how the carbon cycle works. As in all other forests, 50 percent of the dry weight of tree species and peat mosses in the boreal forest is carbon. Trees grow by absorbing carbon dioxide from the atmosphere. The carbon dioxide combines with water and through photosynthesis is eventually converted to sugars, carbohydrates, and cellulose to compose and sustain the plant's organic body. The trees then die, or drop leaves and branches to the forest floor, where they accumulate over time. As long as the carbon remains stored within the plant, it is considered a sink, or a reservoir. But when trees burn or decompose—and when peat bogs burn—they release carbon dioxide back into the atmosphere. The carbon cycle is considered to be in balance when the carbon absorbed by living things is roughly equal to that released by fire and rotting.

Apart from its trees, peatlands, and common mosses, the boreal forest is distinctive for its thousands of lichen species; scientists often refer to the boreal forest as an "open lichen woodland." A lichen is a composite, symbiotic organism made up of a fungus and an alga. The fungus, incapable of making its own food, relies on the alga to manufacture food through photosynthesis. In turn, the alga relies on the fungus for water.

Lichens can be found on bare rocks, dead wood, animal bones, rusty metal, and living bark. They tend to grow in remote areas of the natural world that are too harsh for other organisms. Given the right conditions—adequate light and moisture, clean air, and freedom from competing species—lichens can grow on almost any undisturbed surface.

Lichens are the dominant vegetation on 8 percent of the earth's terrestrial surface. Because they are extremely vulnerable to changes in habitat, the greatest diversity of lichen species can be found in the remnants of ancient forests and other undisturbed ecosystems. That's why they're so common in the boreal forest. In the Laurentian region of Quebec, for example, lichens are so plentiful that they form vast continuous mats on the ground, providing an important source of food for animals. The caribou, one of the most common boreal mammal species, depend on lichens for carbohydrates. In the winter, the witches' hair that blows down from tree canopies during storms provides much-needed sustenance for the black-tailed deer when other lichen species are buried under snow.

In addition, lichens are also a source of medicine; it is estimated that 50 percent of lichen species have antibiotic properties. They have been used to treat illnesses from lung disease and rabies to the common cold.

Lichens play an important role in monitoring the health of the boreal ecosystem itself. They are like sponges, absorbing whatever passes over them through the air. Many species serve as nitrogen fixers, releasing nitrogen for use by vascular plants, and they help control soil erosion. Because of their slow growth rate and their sensitivity to atmospheric conditions, lichens have been used by scientists to study topics from glacial retreat patterns to air pollution levels. This latter function has gained in importance as industrial activity in the boreal forest takes its toll on surrounding forest landscapes. In the mid-1980s, lichens were used to measure the impact of the Chernobyl nuclear disaster. More recently, lichen specimens taken from Alaska's Tongass National Forest were chemically analyzed to determine what toxins were in the air. Downwind of the smoke plume from the Sitka pulp mill, no lichens survived at all.

The boreal ecosystem also has abundant berries. The most common are cranberry, blueberry, strawberry, and cloudberry (a peat bog variety that provided the natural source for *llaka,* a potent, brandylike drink popular in ancient Finland). In the bogs and on the forest floors of some boreal regions, there are carpets of wild twinflower. Other boreal shrubs include Labrador tea— common in cold acid bogs and on wet shores—and fireweed, a honey-producing plant that's one of the first to sprout after a fire or clearing.

Many of these berries and boreal shrubs are loaded with medicinal properties. Labrador tea, for example, is a traditional sedative among indigenous peoples. Good for treating bronchitis and kidney infections, it can also be used to soothe itchy, dry, or chapped skin; to heal burns, blisters, and wounds; and to repel insects or rodents. Some boreal regions are especially rich in healing herbs: in the Russian Far East, more than two hundred medicinal plants can be found in the forests along the Bikin River.

The boreal forest's vast landscape and remote location offer a peaceful home to a large variety of animal species. Throughout the green halo, several types of bear, wolf, deer, and beaver roam the woods. In northwestern Russia and parts of Scandinavia, the reindeer are so plentiful that the indigenous Sámi people have been herders for centuries. The reindeer is not only a source of food during long winters but also an important source of transport, clothing, and sewing materials.

Along the Sweden-Norway border in the south live Norway's largest beasts of prey—brown bear, moose, lynx, wolverine, and wolf. And in Canada, the woodland caribou—closely related to the reindeer—is one of the most enduring symbols of the North.

But many boreal mammals are currently endangered. The Siberian, or Amur, tiger is the most famous of the taiga's threatened species—only an estimated 250 of the world's largest cats still exist in the wild. But the Far Eastern leopard is even rarer; at last count, only thirty of these cats were left along the border between North Korea and China. Russia's Far East is also home to rare species such as the forest cat and the red wolf. In the Siberian taiga, endangered species include the snow leopard, Argali mountain sheep, and red wolf.

In Canada, many of the woodland caribou living in the south have been forced to retreat northward in response to the pressures of development. In recognition of this problem, Ontario has a provincial park specifically devoted to preserving the woodland caribou. Other endangered boreal species in Canada include the wood bison and the black-backed shrew. Although the shrew is not the most exotic of species, it plays a crucial role in the boreal cycle. By dining on the larvae of the larch sawfly, it contributes to insect control in some coniferous forests.

The boreal forest is a treasure trove of bird species. More than two hundred species of birds are found in the western Canadian boreal forest alone. The most common are the bright-colored wood warblers (which include a number of endangered species, such as the Cape May and the Blackburnian). Others include the boreal owl, great gray owl, northern hawk owl, and yellow rail. Among the bird species in the Canadian boreal forest, only 25 percent remain over winter. Many, such as the greater yellowlegs and Cape May warbler, breed in the boreal forest but spend winters in Latin America.

Norwegian pine forests provide an excellent habitat for rare bird species such as the whitebacked woodpecker, the white-tailed sea eagle (Norway has more than 50 percent of the European population), and the gray-headed woodpecker. The endangered peregrine falcon is found in the Siberian taiga, and northeastern Yakutia is home to about eight hundred Siberian cranes—a good portion of the world's population of this threatened species. Luckily, the Kytalyk Resource Reserve, which provides a home for Siberian cranes, is mostly protected territory.

THE UNKNOWN FOREST

> *In typical northern stories, there is no actual acceptance of life and hence, paradoxically, a frequently disinterested gusto and ease in evoking it. The Wilds are grim, yes, the Barrens may claim your life; bad men and wild animals abound.*
>
> —Raymond Knister, from the foreword to
> *Canadian Short Stories* (1928)

Unlike the temperate and tropical rain forests to the south, the boreal forest is still relatively unknown among the public. The current state of the forest and the alarming rate of industrial exploitation going on within its boundaries have yet to inspire the level of urgency that can produce international boycotts and attract pop music celebrities to lobby for the preservation of the Brazilian rain forest. And, unlike the forest ecologists of temperate and tropical zones, many scientists who study the boreal region have toiled in obscurity for decades.

Despite the importance of their work—monitoring the progress of climate change and forest fire patterns, tracking the effects of industrial activity—the research of boreal ecologists has too often fallen on deaf ears in the media, their papers read only by other scientists. Sadly, the people most qualified to inform the public appear to have been silenced by their own expertise—condemned to speak only to each other in a perpetual dialogue of the converted. As a result, public perception of the boreal forest has remained as frozen as the flat, barren tundra of the northern transition zone that many of us mistakenly presume the taiga to be.

How did this happen? Why is there so little public awareness about the boreal forest? Why do so many otherwise educated residents of the South react with blank stares at the mention of the word "boreal"? (Or, more typically, mistake the word "taiga" for "tiger" when combined with the word "Siberian"?)

The most obvious answer is the region's remote geography and extreme seasonal conditions. The boreal forest is notorious for its long winters and inaccessible landscape. Because of the cold weather, boreal trees tend to be less majestic than the towering Douglas-fir. They lack what some eco-activists call the "charismatic mega-flora" of the rain forest—those gigantic trees that make for such stunning visuals on glossy brochures.

Public perception of the boreal forest has remained as frozen as the flat, barren tundra of the northern transition zone that many of us mistakenly presume the taiga to be.

In addition, the nature of the news media has all but guaranteed the taiga's anonymity. To reach the largest possible audience, stories published in newspapers or broadcast on television and radio require immediate news value and a good lead or hook—a dramatic new development on a topic already understood by a general audience. Because the long-term effect of human activity on a forest is difficult to measure—and because the environmental havoc resulting from climate change is a long, gradual process that few of us can fully comprehend—the real newsworthy events in the boreal forest over the last few decades have only recently come to light. And that's largely because the catastrophic nature of those events—the increase in out-of-control wildfires and other symptoms of climate change, for example—are too sensational for the media to ignore.

The media are not alone in neglecting the boreal forest. The region's remoteness, isolation, biting insects, and cold weather have also deterred many gifted scientists from doing research there. As University of Manitoba zoologist William O. Pruitt once lamented:

> The sheer distances involved in the North mean that supply lines for boreal research parties and stations may be long and expensive. Aircraft charter and freight charges frequently make up major items in budgets for northern research. In some instances, fund-granting agencies have rejected worthwhile proposals for field research because they did not appreciate the necessity of the high costs involved. These deterrents mean that boreal ecologists are relatively few and, perforce, dedicated.

Pruitt himself is one of the dedicated few. More than twenty years after writing these words, the septuagenarian zoologist was still leading students young enough to be his grandchildren on grueling survival courses in the frozen taiga. An Arctic field scientist driven by an obsession with snow and its effect on plant and animal life, the former Virginia farm boy has resided in the boreal forest since the 1950s—drawn by its seductive potential as a teaching laboratory. No other scientific discipline, Pruitt writes in *Boreal Ecology*, "can offer such extra attractions as encounters with 'The Throng' of thousands of migrating caribou that vibrate the very earth with their footfalls, or the glimpse of a great bull moose trotting through the golden-leaved aspens on a bright autumn day, or the skin-prickling sound of a wolf's song from a moonlight-flooded taiga hillside."

Today, Pruitt is something of a boreal cult figure. As the author of such books as the classic *Wild Harmony: The Cycle of Life in the Northern Forest*, the founder of the University of Manitoba's Taiga Biological Station, and a recipient of the 1989 federal Northern Science Award, he is that rarest of creatures: a native of the temperate zone who actually prefers a cold climate, who even keeps a bumpersticker on his office door that reads: STAMP OUT SUMMER. But Pruitt's has been a lonely mission in which the requirements of scientific inquiry (a focus on the specific, a need to keep up with new research developments) have prevented him from contributing to popular literature about the boreal forest or from mounting a public-awareness campaign about it.

Another pioneering boreal figure is the Norwegian philosopher Arne Naess. At the Taiga Rescue Network conference in Estonia, Naess remarks: "If you go into a forest of some dimension, after a while you have forest in all directions, and you feel you are in the heart of it." In an essay, he writes: "You look one way, 'forest, forest, forest ... ,' you look another way, 'forest, forest, forest, FOREST.' The forest fills your mind; you are not a subject and the forest is not an object. The dualism is overcome."

Arne Naess is in his 80s now. But when the renowned conservationist talks to a group of activists about the boreal forests of Norway, his eyes light up and his stooping body adopts the expansive gestures of a child. All his life, trees have told him things—expressed their moods to him, just as people do. When he was a small boy, he recalls, two large pine trees were just outside his bedroom window. During the winter when the winds picked up, the trees would sway back and forth, frightening him with their body language. "They told me I was damned—*damned.* I was desperate, so I had a terrible time in relation to those trees, two or three of them. But what was important was that they told me things."

As a teenager, he once took a train from Oslo traveling north. Sitting by the window, he spent hours watching the passing forest, interpreting the trees. Years later, one early morning, he would convince about a hundred people at a lecture in Tokyo to leave the city and accompany him into the woods, about 40 kilometers (25 miles) away. The group stood in the forest for about an hour, saying nothing, just listening to the trees. "Of course, I wanted them to train themselves," he says. "It takes training to see that each tree talks about something different. Each tree is in a different mood."

Naess was encouraging the group to embrace what he calls spontaneous experience, a heightened state of awareness that can only be achieved by seeing the significance of a moment that lasts only tenths of a second. "Very few people have the training to continue having that experience for some seconds and try to articulate what they saw," says Naess. "Poets are able to make two pages of an experience that spontaneous. Most of us cannot articulate, and if we do, not like a poet."

> *"It takes training to see that each tree talks about something different. Each tree is in a different mood."*
>
> —Arne Naess

For those who can, however, this ability heightens sensitivity toward one's own surroundings. For Naess, it has made the gradual deforestation of land surrounding his Norwegian capital all the more painful. The effects are as clear to him in nature as on the color-coded road maps that indicate levels of development. One color on the map represents land that is more than 5 kilometers (3 miles) from the nearest road. Over the years, that color has vanished from each new edition of the map as the city of Oslo develops outward.

"When I was a tiny child," Naess says, "you could go skiing to the center of Oslo, the biggest city in Norway. Then you had to stop ten minutes before the center, then fifteen minutes, then twenty minutes. Then you started using a car for ski trips." One forest near his home had about three hundred trees in a triangle, unbroken by roads. Then the government decided to wipe out the forest to build a school and a road. Naess has seen it all before: the forest sacrificed to extend the capital concentrically, in all directions. The rationale is always the same: "Don't worry—it's only a small piece of land with hardly any trees, not a real forest."

These days, he feels lucky to have a forest right outside his front door. More than twice a week, he still ventures into it, carrying a knapsack to get logs for the woodstove. It's a comforting ritual, combining this practical purpose with the aesthetic experience of being together with the forest. "This *being together* is a very important term," he concludes. "You are not looking out, but you are together with the forest, together with the trees."

It's a kind of relationship to the land that forest people in the taiga have handed down through the generations.

CHAPTER 2

The Forest People

*Many Indians say that their contribution to the ways in which
we live in the future might be far greater than can now be
imagined ... In the end, they may have to teach us the crucial
lessons of survival.*

—Hugh Brody, *Maps and Dreams*

*Southeastern Manitoba
November 11, 1998*

About a two hours' drive north of the city, nestled in a boreal
woodland just east of Manitoba's Lake Winnipeg, lies a tiny out-
post known as the Hollow Water Reserve. Like most Native
communities resulting from the Canadian Indian Act, it's an
impoverished place. Many of its residents depend on welfare.
Although the surrounding forest is controlled by a pulp-and-
paper company, few job opportunities exist for local people. Like
most indigenous residents of the boreal zone, the people of Hollow Water—one of four Ojibway-speaking groups in the region
that form the Anishanaabe First Nation—have lived on this land
since before recorded history. So it seems ironic that on this cold
and snowy Remembrance Day—an annual holiday tribute to war
veterans the Canadian government never fails to observe—I'm
here to break bread with a forgotten people.

Garry Raven is a trapper and former gold miner who has overcome poverty and alcohol abuse to become a productive member

of his community. To the Pine Falls Paper Company, which controls the economy in this region, he is also a force to be reckoned with; not long ago, he organized a successful campaign to overturn a decision granting Pine Falls a two-year logging license that would have given the company year-round access to much of the forest surrounding the reserve.

Garry Raven lives in a wood-framed chalet, deep in the forest, about 30 meters (100 feet) uphill from the Wanipigow River. Stands of poplar and birch surround the house, and a plume of smoke from the chimney rises gently into the still morning air.

At first glance, Raven's world seems a convenient marriage of the old and the new. On one hand, he's a successful trapper, having earned most of his income in the traditional manner of his people. On the other hand, he has incorporated many of the white man's toys into his life. The two snowmobiles sitting in his backyard aren't much of a surprise. In the last three decades, the snowmobile has become a staple of the boreal bush economy. Raven also has a brand-new computer and a large-screen television set, with a boxful of the latest Hollywood videos sitting beside it. He runs the only video rental outlet in Hollow Water.

But the snowmobiles and computer and television set are mere creature comforts. The real world Garry Raven inhabits, and to whose revival he is dedicated, is the traditional world of the Anishanaabe people—glimpses of which can be found in the paintings of warriors, potlatches, and family scenes that adorn most of his living room wall. It's a world that comes to life in the stories he tells. When Raven speaks of his culture, he creates images of a way of life that vanished long ago.

First, he tells me how Hollow Water got its name. According to local elders, it used to be known as Hole River because of a point near the bay where the Bloodvein River empties out to form a whirlpool. This area was the hole in the river, elders say, that once swallowed a boat. According to legend, a local aboriginal man was on his way to a traditional ceremony when he was grabbed by a snake as he was swimming across the river. When the snake began dragging him toward the hole, a thunderbird flew down from a nearby cliff to rescue the man. Instead, the bird was pulled—along with the man and the snake—into the hole. Not long after, locals passing by this part of the river could hear the "hollow" sound of the trapped thunderbird, trying to get out. That's where the name Hollow Water comes from.

"The story goes that the only way we're going to get that thunderbird out of there is by working as a unit," says Raven. "They figure the other reason why it's stuck down there is because of the people, the way we're not working together. By uniting—that's what this elder told me—we're the ones that are going to free the thunderbird."

Until the Pine Falls Paper Company arrived in the early 1930s, Anishanaabe people from neighboring communities used to gather for seasonal ceremonies on sacred grounds not far from Raven's home. One sacred area, just across from Hollow Water, was Manitou-Minis. Translated from Ojibway, the name means "God's Island"—a place where ceremonies were held and big decisions were made by the elders. Now, it's called Black Island—an ironic response, perhaps, to the Christian missionaries who dubbed it "Devil's Island" because of its so-called pagan rituals.

"Black Island was one of the central meeting areas a long, long time ago," says Raven. "All the reserves from four directions came together to meet at Black Island. They discussed how they wanted to work among themselves, how they wanted to teach their youth, how they wanted to exchange medicines—a lot of things. Whatever they had to do, that was their meeting place, where they made their government policy. If you were a chief, this was where you were given your directions on what to do." Another sacred ground not far away, called White Shell, was where sweat lodges, wild rice harvesting, and other traditional ceremonies were held. These ceremonies attracted people from well beyond the region, including the United States.

Hollow Water was once rich in medicinal plants. Now, the plants are much weaker as a result of industrial pollution, but they're still there. Raven keeps several varieties in his kitchen: juniper, cranberry, Labrador tea, sweetgrass, balsam, poplar, tamarack. The list goes on. "In some cases, like the blueberry, you can eat them like that, but you can also make juices out of them. Using water with crushed berries has a natural strength—no preservatives added."

Later, talking with Garry's brother, Raymond, I learn a little Anishanaabe secret about gender and ecology. The poplar, says Raymond, is the first tree to grow in the springtime. "It's just like the hair of Mother Earth," he tells me. "When she's bald somewhere, and you experience somewhere that hasn't been clear-cut, the first thing that will grow is poplar, because She has to move fast to protect herself, to hold whatever is there."

All of nature, he says, is a union of male and female elements. Even water. "Female water," he says, pointing out the window at a snowdrift, "is all this water that's sitting on the earth." It nurtures the soil, protecting plant and even some animal species from the cold the way a womb protects a fetus. "What's up there when it rains, when it falls," he adds, pointing skyward, "that's the male water." It fertilizes, it plants, it imposes itself. "We experience that every spring."

Raymond pauses for a few moments as he looks out the window at the snowdrift. "When I was young I was always [asked] 'What did the First Nations ever contribute to this country?' I didn't know. But as I found my culture, I could see the biggest contribution our culture ever gave this [country] was medicine. And that's what our people are saying: we have to preserve all this medicine."

Raymond's elders anticipate a time in the not-too-distant-future when the modern medical system will face a crisis because of privatization and the overpricing of drugs. When that happens, pharmaceutical companies will rush to exploit traditional medicines. "When my dad was dying, medicines were taken from this area to the hospital and he was given this medicine," he recalls. "In a few days, he was hopping around. And the doctors there, the nurses there, wanted to analyze what was put in that medicine. I said 'Well, it's not going to work for you, because the way we do it is that medicine is put away for a ceremony for it to work. It's the guy up there [the Creator] that makes it work; it's not us.'"

What will happen if the medical industry turns to herbal remedies? I ask him. "It won't work that way," he smiles, "because whatever they take, they turn into powder. All our medicines are given in liquid."

Later that day, Garry's son Robert takes me on a half-hour drive to the site where he and his father, along with Don Sullivan and another friend, are gathering firewood. As the late-afternoon darkness arrives, an eerieness settles in. Forests can be pretty desolate places in the first decade or so after a major fire. Stretched before me is an endless stand of black stalks, burnt offerings in a seemingly barren landscape.

*Around the world, more than a
million indigenous people live in the taiga.*

Returning home with the last truckload of firewood—we've done three loads by suppertime—Garry tells me why he goes into the burned forest to get his firewood. "A lot of people, when they want their firewood, they go into the living forest to get it," he tells me, shaking his head. "Why don't they just come here? It's perfectly good firewood, and you're not killing anything to get it." Gazing out of his truck window, I catch a glimpse of one hefty, charred trunk as we pass by. He's right, I tell him: "These burnt trees are just *waiting* to be plucked."

Garry Raven's campaign to save the forest, prompted by a half-century legacy of industrial impacts by the Pine Falls Paper Company, will wait for another chapter. For now, the story of my brief visit to Hollow Water can serve as a glimpse into the lives of one aboriginal community in the boreal forest. Around the world, more than a million indigenous people live in the taiga. Other Canadian Native peoples include the Dene of Yukon and the Northwest Territories; the Cree of the Prairies, Ontario, and Quebec; and the Innu of Newfoundland. The Sámi people can be found in Norway, Sweden, Finland, and western Russia; the Even and Komi in the Sakha Republic; the Nenets, Yakut, Udege, and Altaisk in Siberia; and the Ainu in northern Japan. For many of these people, and others who have settled for centuries in the green halo, the forest is a sacred place whose gifts provide life and whose resources can never be "owned."

TRADITIONAL ENVIRONMENTAL KNOWLEDGE: THE WAY OF THE LAND

For some years now, anthropologists and historians have been using the term "traditional knowledge" or "traditional environmental knowledge" to describe the wisdom of aboriginal people whose lived experience in the "bush" has been passed down through the generations. In its aboriginal context, the word "traditional" could best be defined as a "preference for country foods, ability to hunt and prepare meat or hides, capacity for finding one's way in the bush, and willingness to share what one has. For many it also means knowledge of one or more Indian languages" and, in some parts of the bush, "considerable skill on horseback." Traditional environmental knowledge, in essence, is wisdom based on memory and experience of the same natural environment over an extended period of time. It means making a long-term investment in one's community and resources.

Until fairly recently, academia, industry, and even some parts of the conservation movement tended to view undeveloped forest landscapes from an exclusively ecological perspective. Such land-scapes were considered "wilderness" territory, which—depending on your point of view—should be destined for parkland or the sawmill. Such land was considered devoid of human presence, even if hunters and gatherers, fishers, or reindeer herders were living there. "Environments used by non-agricultural peoples are now seen not as 'wilderness' areas but as cultural landscapes that have been used over a long period," writes Inga-Maria Mulk, a Swedish expert on the Sámi reindeer herders of Scandinavia and Russia. "The landscape is perceived as dynamic and acquires meaning solely through the actions of the people using it."

One study showed how the James Bay Cree of central Canada help the boreal forest stay in balance by serving as natural preda-tors of certain animal populations:

> The decision on where to harvest and what species to harvest is made so that harvest levels are greatest when the animals are abundant. For example, beaver are harvested primarily from areas where trappers observe depletion of the beaver's food supply, but after an area is trapped for 2–4 years, it is left untrapped for 6–10 years, or until there is again evidence of overbrowsing … The respect shown for animals means that each hunter harvests only what is needed, with minimal "over-harvest" and waste.

In nonaboriginal systems, the rigid application of supply-and-demand economics can wipe out an animal stock or a fishery altogether. The Pacific sardine and Peruvian anchovy fisheries are just two examples in which an increase in harvesting levels (in response to declining populations) led to a complete collapse of the stock. Compared with this approach, the Cree method is a model of sustainable harvesting.

For the Cree and other Native peoples, the forest, like other types of ecosystem, is an extension of the indigenous person's own life. As one Sámi person put it, after being arrested for opposing the construction of a dam in Norway's Lapland: "If you dam this river, you will hurt me, because this river is part of me."

The Reindeer People

Can the survival of an entire indigenous culture depend on the fate of an animal species? In the case of the Sámi people of Scandinavia and Russia, there's good reason to think so. For the Sámi, the reindeer is much more than simply a source of food and raw materials. This symbol of the North is one of the last cultural staples protecting Sámi settlements from industrial encroachment, Sámi languages from extinction, and the people themselves from final assimilation into the southern economy and culture.

The Sámi people, often known as Laplanders, are settled in the Lapland region of northern Finland and Sweden and on the Kola Peninsula of northwestern Russia. Some anthropologists discourage the use of the word "Lapp" or "Laplander" to refer to the Sámi. Because the word "Lapp" can be translated to mean a patch of cloth for mending, it is thought that the application of this term to the Sámi—who use reindeer hides for clothing—carries a derogatory connotation (like "hobo" or "tramp"). Also, the word "Laplander" can refer to anyone who lives in the region, including non-Native people. As such, the term does not recognize the Sámi people who live outside the Lapland region. Today, the total Sámi population is about 51,000. (The breakdown is Norway: 30,000; Sweden: 15,000; Finland: 4000; Russia: 2000.) Sámi Laplanders have their own parliament, as well as separate schools, newspapers, and daily public radio broadcasts. They also publish books and records in the Sámi language. Sámi communities are scattered throughout the Scandinavian coast from Norway (which also has its own Sámi parliament) to northwestern Russia.

Sámi culture is distinct from other Nordic cultures. In Finland, three dialects of Sámi are spoken—the language is related to the Finnish tongue. But the dialects, spoken from Norway to Russia, are so different from one end of the Sámi nation to another that they are mutually incomprehensible. Sámi handicrafts date back several centuries. Sámi narrative tradition, passed down through the generations by storytelling, is famous for its use of *yoiking,* a form of chanting.

When a Sámi physical landscape is violated by the mining industry, it's more than just resources that are plundered—it's cultural memory as well.

The chief cultural differences between the Sámi and non-aboriginal Nordic people lie in how they see the landscape. The Sámi consider the land sacred because it is inhabited by ancestors and contains cultural traces of all that has happened there before. It exists "in people's memories and imaginations, and [is] connected to place names, myth and folklore." Like people in most indigenous cultures throughout the world, the Sámi don't distinguish between the visible and invisible parts of a landscape as readily as southern, non-Native people do. They are just as likely to see the landscape in the stories, myths, and legends of their community as they are in the directly observable fields of rock carvings, hearths and cooking pits, reindeer-herding fences, and grave sites. One of those landscapes is Apar Mountain, in Sarek National Park, which, according to Sámi folklore, is where the voices of the spirits of dead children can be heard. Such stories create "mental maps" that allow the Sámi to pass on their cultural values from one generation to the next. So when a Sámi physical landscape is violated by the mining industry, it's more than just resources that are plundered—it's cultural memory as well.

One of the largest Sámi communities is in Lapland, one of the milder regions of the Arctic, where the northernmost forests in the world can be found. Covered with huge pine forests, the taiga hills of Finland are a perfect habitat for the reindeer, whose role in this culture predates recorded history. For centuries, reindeer herding, along with fishing and hunting, has been considered by law to be a traditional livelihood. A model of sustainable resource use, the Sámi tradition of herding always makes maximum use of the reindeer. All parts of the carcass are eaten, including the intestines, which provide important vitamins that are hard to come by for much of the year. Although milking is seldom practiced anymore, reindeer tendons and sinews are still used for sewing everything from shoes and clothing to cone-shaped tents. Live reindeer are also used as a form of transport.

Today, the state of Finland owns more than 90 percent of the area in the Sámi region. Throughout the 20th century, the government opened so much of the land to mining, clear-cut logging, oil exploration, and hydroelectric power operations that reindeer habitat has diminished dramatically. As a result, much of the Sámi population has been forced to rely on nontraditional sources of income. In some cases, entire families have uprooted and moved south to seek work, setting up shop in big cities such as Stockholm or Oslo. (One joke among the Sámi refers to Stockholm as the largest Sámi colony in the world.)

The Reindeer Husbandry Law of 1971 did grant the Sámi people some rights to land and water within their traditional territory. It established herding districts varying in size from 1000 to 5000 square kilometers (400 to 2000 square miles) throughout Scandinavia. But no such rights were granted to Sámi hunters and fishers. Thus, the reindeer has become symbolic of the Sámi's struggle to protect their culture.

Most Sámi now have at least one relative or friend connected to the reindeer economy. But even this last remaining link to the Sámi's indigenous tradition is being threatened. The reindeer-herding districts have come under increasing pressure from Russian oil exploration, as well as forestry and mining. In recent years, the Sámi have gone to court to prevent clear-cut logging on traditional lands, suing the Finnish Forest and Parks Service, which controls logging on state land. So far, the Sámi have lost every case.

BOREAL SPIRIT: THE FOREST AS TEMPLE

Estonia, site of the 4th Taiga Rescue Network conference in fall 1998, is the northernmost of the three Baltic states and one of the oldest nations in Europe. Estonian people are said to have lived in the region for nearly nine thousand years—as far back as the last ice age. Their ancestors, the Finno-Ugrians, were the first people to arrive in the boreal forest of Europe and western Siberia, about a thousand years ago. The Finno-Ugrian empire of nations was much larger than today's European Union, but not many remnants of the culture exist. One of the few is the Estonian tradition of the "forest people."

The Finno-Ugrians practiced what we would now call a forest religion. All plants, animals, and other living creatures—even the forest itself—were said to have a soul. Forests were full of supernatural powers. "Their authority and influence on people of that time was stronger than the authority of forest protection laws or police today," according to Hendrik Relve, an Estonian forest activist. Before the arrival of Christianity, all cultures had some kind of nature worship. Because Finno-Ugrians lived in the forests, the tree was the most important part of everyday life and therefore the most important object of worship.

Sacred trees, and the taboos surrounding them, were a big part of their faith. "One of the rules that was very strict was that you had to completely avoid touching a sacred forest," says Relve. "If you harmed a sacred object, you were punished." About a century ago, there used to be a sacred wood not far from Relve's home, a short drive south of the Estonian capital of Tallinn. One day, a man wandering through the wood took a branch from the forest home with him. Shortly afterward, he fell sick. Convinced that he was being punished for blasphemy, he returned the branch to the forest. Another man, needing some timber to build a fence for his cows, cut some trees from the same wood. Soon after, all his cows died. Another man who cut down a sacred tree went blind. Since the 19th century, according to Relve, "our folklorists have collected lots of stories about people who take care to avoid touching the sacred trees but have forgotten why they are afraid of touching them."

In recent years, skeptics have argued that the number of sacred trees in Estonia increased dramatically during the country's national awakening in the early 20th century. Apparently, the sentiment inspired by forest religion had become a form of opportunism—an ideological tool in the fight for independence. With the passing of Estonia's first nature protection laws in 1935, the people's fear of punishment by supernatural powers was replaced by fear of earthly powers such as the state. Nevertheless, the present attitude of Estonians toward the forest and the trees is to some extent influenced by ancient taboos.

PEOPLE AS PART OF THE FOREST

During the Taiga Rescue Network conference, one of the delegates I sat down with was a young woman from an indigenous group called the Even, one of more than eighty ethnic groups in the Russian republic of Yakutia. Natalia Cherbakova's people have lived in the area for thousands of years. Born and raised in a Yakutia settlement, Cherbakova was now living in Moscow and attending the Russian Academy of Sciences. When I met her, she was writing her graduate dissertation on the iconographical calendar of the Even people. Through a translator, she told me how the Even have used religious customs to live in harmony with the forest.

According to Even custom, there are three worlds: lower, middle, and higher. "The forest, like people, is born in the middle world," said Cherbakova. "The spirit is the higher world, where all the gods are." The lower world is the world of the dead. The

Even are not bound by dualistic thinking, so flora and fauna are not divided into good versus bad, necessary or unnecessary. Both are equally important, and humanity is responsible for taking care of them. When the Even divide up a hunted deer, they cut the carcass in a way that minimizes bleeding, thus showing respect for the deer. It's forbidden to cut down larch trees, because they're holy. And not only is clear-cutting a forest bad for the environment—it's a mortal sin.

According to Even tradition, the people themselves are an integral part of the forest. In pre-Christian times, this belief could be witnessed in the Even custom of "burying" the dead in trees. A bag was sewn out of fur or a pelt, the corpse was inserted in the fetal position, and then the bag was tied very tightly and placed between branches quite high in the tree, where animals couldn't reach it. These tree cemeteries were forbidden protected zones, or sacred ground, for the Even. "We were not allowed to go there," Cherbakova told me, "because we'd be disturbing their rest."

The Even also have two holy larch trees: "Between these two larches they tie a rope, and we cannot go beyond there because that's considered a road to the higher world." Only during the New Year's celebration, during the native Dance of the Sun, are people allowed to move between the two trees. At any other time, they might risk banishment to the lower world.

Some might say the Even are disappearing anyway. Indigenous language was the first casualty of what Cherbakova calls the Yakutia-ization of her people. Because the Yakuts needed a larger population to form a republic, she argues, the Russian government gradually phased out any common use of minority languages in the region that ultimately became the republic. It was a benign but deliberate form of linguistic ethnic cleansing. The situation has improved lately; more Even books are being published, and an Even representative serves in the Russian Duma. But it's a struggle. The federal government's *Status of Indigenous Peoples Report*, for example, lacks teeth. "There's no law about land use or traditional resource use, and this is already the sixth year where [Russia] hasn't passed a law," according to Cherbakova. "They're ignoring us. They often tell me, when I visit the Duma or the White House, things like 'It would be better if there were fewer of you. In fact it would be better if there were none of you at all, because then the resources would all be ours.' It's not advantageous for them that Native people control their own land."

---

*According to Even tradition, the people themselves
are an integral part of the forest.*

Sitting beside me during our conversation was Olga Galchinova, a Russian ethnographer. Galchinova has done a lot of work with the indigenous peoples of the Komi Republic. The virgin Komi forests are the largest intact old-growth forests in the continent. The Komi people constitute 23 percent of the republic's population of 1.25 million. Three-quarters of the indigenous peoples speak the Komi language, a Finno-Ugric tongue. And like the Even, the Komi have an ancient connection to their land.

Each Komi family has its own section of forest, a plot of land handed down through the generations. As a result, the territory hasn't been disrupted. It's a philosophy at odds with the Russian view of resource "planning," says Galchinova. "People feel a greater responsibility to the territory where they live, and to their descendants."

Like the Even tradition, Komi spiritual tradition places a high value on nature. But there is less fear attached to the forest. "It surprised me when I talked to the Komi that they didn't tell any terrible stories about forest spirits," says Galchinova. "From birth, a child doesn't have a fear of the forest. The forest is part of the child, and vice versa. They are not taught to fear the forest, with stories of terrible, evil forest spirits."

Instead, the Komi emphasize the healing properties of nature. Spring water is especially potent, says Galchinova: "The Komi believe that spring water heals all illnesses. In some places, the springs are considered the tears of legends. If a woman from another nationality drinks this water, she must marry one of these people. A spring can predict the fate of a person. If you throw some coins into a spring and the water bubbles, you will have a happy life. After ten o'clock at night, it's forbidden to go to the river, because the river is very tired from boats and people, and needs to rest during the night."

Such customs may seem quaint to the modern reader, but they contain a wisdom that should not be discounted. The boreal region of the Even and the Komi people is ecologically sustainable because it fosters a custodial approach to resources and their protection. In some cases, the survival of a culture itself depends on the fate of those resources.

CHAPTER 3

Taiga, Taiga, Burning Bright

Give me seven dry days in the boreal forest, and you'll soon see a raging fire.

—Michael Flannigan, Canadian Forestry Service research
scientist, quoted in the *Globe and Mail*

During the spring and summer of 1998, the people of Edmonton, Alberta, awoke each morning to find the sky above them filled with billowing black clouds of acrid smoke. Dozens of fires blazed out of control north of the provincial capital, consuming more than 300,000 hectares (740,000 acres) of wild boreal forest. As the smoky fires turned the prairie sky into an endless night, newspaper headlines screamed, "Alberta burns." It was one of the worst fires in recent memory for this western Canadian province, which had seen its share of record blazes. But it was a mere brush fire compared with what was going on halfway around the world near Khabarovsk, a city of 620,000 located just north of the Chinese border in the Russian Far East.

By mid-October, at least 2000 square kilometers (800 square miles) of forest—an area equal to the size of Switzerland—had gone up in flames, and another 1.7 million hectares (4.2 million acres) was still burning. As much as 50 million tonnes of carbon gases had been released into the atmosphere. United Nations experts visiting Khabarovsk called it a global disaster area.

Forest fires have always been a regular feature of the boreal nature cycle, but the fires in Alberta and Khabarovsk appeared to signal a disturbing trend. Each year for the previous three decades, the number and scale of wild fires in the boreal region had increased. By the late 1970s, northern Saskatchewan had lost much of its spruce forest. In 1989 alone, Manitoba lost 4 million hectares (10 million acres)—8 percent of its total forest area. And by the late 1990s, the average annual area burned in all of the Canadian boreal forest had risen from 1 to 3 million hectares (2.5 to 7.4 million acres). Things weren't much better in interior Alaska, where three-quarters of the spruce-birch forest had disappeared by the late seventies. Fire-suppression programs had all but eliminated wild fires in the Scandinavian taiga. But in Siberia —the largest boreal forest in the world—at least 10,000 square kilometers (4000 square miles) of forest were still being eliminated by fires each year. And a growing body of evidence suggested that these fires were being stoked by climate change, human activity, or a combination of both.

NATURAL DISTURBANCE: A LIFE-GIVING DESTRUCTION

As any boreal ecologist will tell you, fire is but one of three main natural disturbances in the boreal forest. Since the last ice age, insect infestation, stormy weather, and fire have all shaped the boreal forest in generational cycles. When all three factors are in balance—that is, when they occur at regular intervals without being affected by climate or human activity—these disturbances are good for the forest. They lead to succession, the regeneration of the forest, which depends on the temperature, moisture, and reproductive ability of the forest. Temperature plays a role in succession because the hotter the climate gets, the harder it is for trees to retain enough carbon to survive. Moisture is important because if a tree loses more water than it can absorb through its roots, it will dehydrate and die. Finally, many boreal tree species require a long period of chilling before warmer spring temperatures trigger budburst and new growth. The higher the spring temperature, the greater the likelihood that trees will produce abnormal or incomplete cones or that they will not be able to reproduce.

Insects, the first natural disturbance, help the forest in a number of subtle ways: decomposing litter and serving as a food supply for birds and small mammals, and sometimes even reducing the chances of catastrophic fire by helping to get rid of old or diseased tree stands. But a rapidly increasing insect population caused by higher temperatures is usually bad news for the living trees of the forest. In eastern Canada, an outbreak of the spruce budworm from 1970 to the mid-1980s caused the defoliation of some 55 million hectares (135 million acres) of forest—an area larger than France. The spruce bark beetle, more common in the Eurasian boreal zone, thrives on trees struck by lightning or disease. Large outbreaks of the bark beetle often occur in areas weakened by windstorms, fires, drought, or budworm attacks. Two large outbreaks occurred on the northern Japanese island of Hokkaido following storm damage caused by typhoons in 1954 and 1981.

Storms and lightning, the second natural disturbance in the boreal life cycle, are especially influential in the maritime regions of northeastern Asia and North America. For example, in the aftermath of a storm, younger forests may spring up and mix with strips of mature tree stands, creating wave forests.

Fires, the third natural disturbance, have a long history in the taiga. Using sediment cores pulled from the bottom of subarctic lakes and bogs, scientists have determined that fires were burning in the Great Bear Lake region of the Northwest Territories at least 7600 years ago. Farther west, core samples show that parts of the Yukon forest burned 9000 years ago.

Depending on the forest, boreal fires occur in cycles that range from 100 to 400 years. Studies show that, on average, major fires occur in Alaskan tree stands once every 50 to 100 years, in eastern Siberia once every 130 years, and in eastern Canada once every

200 years. As a result, boreal forests regularly undergo change. In contrast, temperate rain forests can last for up to 2000 years without any disturbance except for individual trees falling over. Boreal trees just don't have time to gather the huge tufts of moss that look so good in photographs.

Because so much of the boreal forest is composed of highly resinous coniferous trees, it has always been susceptible to fire. Trees such as black and white spruce, balsam fir, and jack pine all tend to litter the forest floor with branches, cones, and other highly flammable material that doesn't easily decompose. Fire releases the nutrients of these materials, providing nourishment that allows seeds to germinate. By burning dead trees and underbrush, fires produce new trees from the charred remains that are often more robust than the older ones they replace. In forests dominated by black spruce, the burning of the thick humous layer produces ashes, which allow the nutrients to return to the soil. This combustion often creates an ideal germination bed for such species as black spruce, white birch, and trembling aspen. In jack pine stands, heat from fire enables the highly resinous cones to open, thereby releasing the seeds. New aspen grows from the roots of old trees—even if the trees are charred—while black spruce and lodgepole pine can keep live seeds in their cones for years, releasing the seeds when the fires attack them.

Fires improve the boreal forest by removing trees weakened by age, drought, storms, or insects. They also play a role in species distribution and age class. When a fire rips through an old forest, the extent of its damage—and the species that fall within its path—often determines how much of the regenerated forest will be an "even-aged" stand and which species will be included. In this way, fires function as a kind of natural housecleaning: out with the old, in with the new.

Some forest industry representatives have argued that clearcuts fulfill a similar function to that of fires. They "mimic nature," in other words, by getting rid of old trees and replacing them through reforestation. The Alberta Forest Products Association, for example, says that clear-cutting "most closely emulates the natural disturbance patterns, particularly fire." This argument has been discredited—largely because fires, unlike clear-cuts, "do not leave behind a network of logging roads, landings and skid trails, creating a long-lasting risk of landslides." Nor do they consume every tree on a site or destroy the diversity of structures left behind.

Fires improve the boreal forest by removing trees weakened by age, drought, storms, or insects.

For all the good they do, however, fires can be devastating to the boreal ecosystem. At the northern margins, fire often melts permafrost and degrades the soil. Elsewhere, it reduces timber production while destroying habitat for caribou, bears, migratory birds, and other plant and animal species. Finally, fires in the southern boreal region create conditions suitable for grassland and set up a competition between forests and grassland. When grasslands win out, lichens are destroyed and animals such as the caribou lose a major source of food. When fires happen more often than once every ten years, few tree species survive—the area usually reverts to grassland.

Fires can also have tragic consequences when combined with toxic waste. In the forests surrounding Bryansk, a Russian city located about 500 kilometers (300 miles) northeast of Chernobyl, the effects of the devastating 1986 nuclear disaster were still being felt a dozen years later. Bryansk has suffered even more radiation pollution than Ukraine, where the accident occurred. The greater pollution in Bryansk is largely due to the increase in forest fires, which have spread radiation fallout even farther through smoke and wind.

The combination of fire, insects, and storms can have devastating effects. Gale-force winds can wreak havoc during forest fires. They trigger a domino effect by blowing down trees and thus creating fuel to turn a small fire into an out-of-control blaze. Storms also spread insect infestation by blowing budworms and beetles for long distances throughout the forest. Fires and insects, in turn, create exposed breaks in the forest that increase the effect of a windstorm. So all three disturbances play off each other to shape the boreal forest. In the 20th century, however, fire outstripped the other two with an astonishing legacy of destruction that is threatening the future of the boreal forest itself.

PLAYING WITH FIRE

For the early indigenous inhabitants of the boreal forest, fire was a practical tool for everyday life. They used it to dry out trails, celebrate special events, and create a more open forest that made it easier to hunt. They used it to thaw snow or frozen ground so that they could collect berries, medicinal herbs, and spruce root. They used it to build and patch birchbark canoes and, finally, to burn the tangled undergrowth that made overland travel impossible.

For all the good they do, however, fires can be devastating to the boreal ecosystem.

With the arrival of European settlers, however, North American boreal fires began to get out of hand. By the end of the 19th century, the boreal forest was overrun with fur traders, missionaries, prospectors, railway builders, loggers, bush rangers, and other explorers whose careless disregard for their new environment became a recipe for disaster. The problem reached a crisis point during the Klondike Gold Rush in summer 1898, when a thousand gold seekers converged on Yukon via Edmonton and the North-west Territories.

Traveling up the Slave and Mackenzie Rivers, passing through the boreal forest's vast network of streams and trails, itinerant panhandlers left countless fires in their wake. The sheer magnitude of the boreal forest must have induced a certain degree of apathy in these travelers, who may have assumed that a small brushfire wouldn't make a large dent in a forest that big.

As civilization gradually encroached on the boreal forest, the fires grew larger and more dangerous. When mining and lumber towns were established in the late 19th century, many of them were incinerated by boreal fires. In 1911, a fire near Timmins, Ontario, burned 200,000 hectares (500,000 acres) of forest and killed 73 people. Five years later, another fire in the same region destroyed several towns and killed 244 people. In 1922, fire destroyed 6000 homes and killed 43 people. In 1929, a fire covering more than 50 square kilometers (19 square miles) nearly engulfed the Northwest Territories community of Fort Smith. One of the biggest fires ever recorded in North America spread from piles of unburned slash the American military had carelessly dumped on the roadside during construction of the Alaska Highway in southern Yukon. In fall 1942, this single blaze consumed an area of forest the size of Ireland, burning as far east as the Mackenzie River. The Northwest Territories also suffered heavy forest fire damage from the military's construction of roads and an oil pipeline across the Mackenzie Mountains. In 1950, another huge blaze—the Great Chinchaga Fire—burned more than a million hectares (2.5 million acres) of forest in northern Alberta.

But not even a growing human presence in the boreal forest over the past century can account for the growing number of wildfires in the past three decades. In the central and western boreal forest of Canada, the decade from 1970 to 1980 showed an increase in warming and drought. The 1980s were the warmest decade on record; the 1990s were even warmer. Around the world, nine of the eleven hottest years in a century and a half of modern record keeping have occurred since 1986.

What has this trend meant for the boreal forest? In the Canadian region, the increase in fires appears to be due to a combination of higher temperatures, a declining rainfall, and aging tree stands. After a devastating fire, the new trees that grow in its wake are all the same age. As a result of such large-scale fires, the Canadian boreal forest contains several patches of older, even-aged stands of trees that are now more susceptible to insects and diseases. Put rather crudely, the life cycle of this current group of trees is like the forest version of the postwar baby boomers, now in the throes of late middle age. Just as we are seeing an increase in cancer rates and a panic about the availability of pension funds in the next quarter century, the "baby boom" of boreal trees is also working its way through the system. And—as with human vulnerability to disease—an aging population of trees is more vulnerable than a younger population to fluctuations in climate.

The 1980s were the warmest decade on record; the 1990s were even warmer. Around the world, nine of the eleven hottest years in a century and a half of modern record keeping have occurred since 1986.

Dr. David W. Schindler, an ecology professor at the University of Alberta, witnessed the increase in fires firsthand during his twenty-two years at a remote research camp in northwestern Ontario. Between 1970 and 1990, temperatures in this region were from 0.8 to 2.0°C (1.4 to 3.6°F) higher than long-term averages. The area burned by forest fires was double the area burned in the previous few decades. "At the research station that I directed during the period, a temperature increase of 1.6 degrees C and a decline of about 50 percent in precipitation caused several massive forest fires in the 1970s and 1980s," he writes. "Some areas were burned twice."

In Khabarovsk in 1998, the seasonal fires that normally occurred following the April drought blazed out of control because the normal rains arrived late, thus prolonging the drought. This drought, combined with a weakened Russian economy that crippled fire-suppression budgets, was a recipe for environmental disaster.

To comprehend the enormous scale of devastation in Khabarovsk, consider that the Siberian taiga where the fires burned stretches for 3.4 million square kilometers (1.3 million square miles) to the far east Pacific coast. Twice the size of the Amazon rain forest, this rich coniferous forest contains about one-quarter of the world's timber reserves. During the three-month period in which the fires were at their peak, an average of 520 hectares (1285 acres) of forest a day went up in flames. The country had already lost massive amounts of income because of illegal logging in the region. The fires only made it easier for smugglers to operate, because authorities were too busy with damage control to monitor already-harvested stocks. The Russian forest industry lost 15 million cubic meters (20 million cubic yards) of high-quality timber—more than three times the annual timber production in Khabarovsk and only 6 million cubic meters (8 million cubic yards) less than the annual allowable cut for all of Russia.

When the fires began to threaten an oil pipeline and a natural gas pipeline leading from the island of Sakhalin to the mainland, the United Nations stepped forward with U.S.$2.5 million in firefighting funds—adding to the U.S.$2.5 million already spent by the cash-strapped region. The rescue effort was not made any easier by Russia's economic crisis. Several firefighting helicopters remained grounded because of the lack of fuel and spare parts. At the same time, the timber industry was losing untold millions of dollars in potential work because of the need to shift resources to fire fighting.

But the cost in human and environmental terms was much harder to measure. At least three people had died in Sakhalin, and eight hundred people were left homeless in September when the village of Gorki burned down. Throughout the region, more than one million people had suffered from the effects of long-term exposure to smoke, including carbon monoxide poisoning. According to a local aboriginal resource center, some pregnant women had to get abortions because their fetuses had died in the womb as a result of exposure to the gas. Carbon dioxide levels in the air surrounding Khabarovsk were so high—twice the normal amount—that residents could taste the soot as they breathed. The smoke was so thick that some firefighting planes couldn't even leave the tarmac at Khabarovsk Airport to douse the flames.

Meanwhile, an animal habitat was disappearing. Fires had reached the Sikhote-Alin Wildlife Reserve, one of the few homes of the endangered Amur tiger, of which only four hundred are left in the world. The tigers, like other animals in the forest, had been forced to move closer to civilization to escape the flames. As a result, they were vulnerable to poachers and starvation. "Even if poachers do not kill all Amur tigers, their population will decrease by several times because they will be deprived of food," an official from the State Ecological Commission told the Environmental News Network. "Then the Amur tiger will disappear forever. And the long, thorough work put into saving this species will be over."

In one apartment building not far from the blazing forest, residents were startled one day to find a brown bear wandering through the lobby. Clearly, nature was trying to tell them something.

CHAPTER 4

Hot and Bothered: Global Warming and the Boreal Forest

We're not going to run out of fossil fuel, we're going to run out of atmosphere to put it into.

—Ecologist Werner Kurz

Global warming reaches Far North

—*Globe and Mail* headline, September 14, 1998

The news was alarming, but it was hard for climate scientists not to feel vindicated. A *Globe and Mail* front page story on September 14, 1998, confirmed what many had predicted three decades earlier—that climate change was an indisputable fact, that the world's higher latitudes were developing unusually high temperatures, and that these changes were beginning to cause problems in the boreal forest.

During a year in which weather stories competed with American presidential sex follies for front page coverage, global warming was one of the top newsmakers. Nineteen ninety-eight was shaping up to be the hottest year on record. Across Canada, the temperature was 2.7°C (4.9°F) above normal, and across the boreal halo the 20th century was promising to be the hottest in six hundred years.

Given the recent symptoms of climate change—record numbers of forest fires, a cycle of hurricanes, storms, and devastating floods—perhaps none of this should have been surprising. More significant was the growing number of scientists who agreed that a major culprit in global warming was the greenhouse effect, exacerbated by an increase in fossil fuel emissions.

THE GREENHOUSE EFFECT
AND FOSSIL FUEL EMISSIONS

Greenhouse gases such as water vapor, carbon dioxide, methane, and nitrous oxide trap heat from the sun, preventing it from being radiated from the earth back into space (see Table 4.1). This phenomenon is known as the greenhouse effect. For millions of years, this effect has prevented the planet from becoming a frozen wasteland. When kept at a natural level, the greenhouse effect sustains the diversity of life on the planet, allowing plants to grow and soils to form. Without it, we'd all be shivering at somewhere between -6°C (21°F) and -18°C (0°F). Instead, the world's temperature has hovered at the more comfortable average of 15°C (60°F).

For many years, a handful of scientists and business lobbyists dismissed the role of greenhouse gases in climate change, calling them mere companions to global warming rather than causes of it. But now, most scientists agree that the increase in greenhouse gases has led to global warming and that much of this increase is due to the rise in fossil fuel consumption by an increasingly industrialized society. Since pre-industrial times, concentrations of carbon dioxide in the atmosphere have gone up 30 percent, with half of that gain occurring in the last three decades of the 20th century. From 1860 to 1997, the world's annual consumption of oil rose from 300 million tonnes to 8730 million tonnes. Today sophisticated new computer models have linked climate change with the 20th century's overconsumption of fossil fuels. The conclusions of these studies are similar to those of studies that tested lake muds, peat deposits, ice cores, and other deposits to track the progress of climate change.

For Jim Bruce, a meteorologist and member of the United

Table 4.1 Greenhouse Gases Targeted for Reduction by Governments

Gas	Source	Duration in Atmosphere	Dangers
Carbon dioxide	Produced naturally by decaying vegetation, animal respiration, and human activities such as fossil fuel burning	120 years	Accounts for 75 percent of Canada's contribution to global warming
Methane	Produced naturally by animals and vegetation decomposition and in petroleum production; is the primary component of natural gas	10 years	Is more powerful than carbon dioxide; has about 21 times the potential for global warming
Nitrous oxide	Produced naturally through decomposition of nitrogen in the soil and by human activities involving the production of fertilizers and fuel combustion	150 years	
Poly-fluorocarbons	Produced as a by-product of aluminum smelting	Varying duration	
Hydro-fluorocarbons	Produced in aerosols and refrigerators	40 to 250 years	
Sulfur hexafluoride	Produced by electrical equipment	3200 years	

(Source: Agence France Presse)

Nations' Intergovernmental Panel on Climate Change (IPCC), the connection between industrial emissions and climate is an undeniable fact. "There are very few, very few [scientists] who will not agree with the proposition that increased greenhouse gas in the atmosphere will cause a gradual warming in the climate," Dr. Bruce told the *Globe and Mail*. Three years earlier, in the carefully worded *Report on the Science of Climate Change*, the IPCC had spoken of the industrial factors driving the forces of climate change:

> Our ability to quantify the human influence on global climate is currently limited because the expected signal is still emerging from the noise of natural variability, and because there are uncertainties in key factors. These include the magnitude and patterns of long-term natural variability and the time evolving pattern of forcing by, and response to, changes in concentrations of greenhouse gases and aerosols, and land surface changes. Nevertheless, the balance of evidence suggests that there is a discernible human influence on global climate.

THE VANISHING HALO: FROM SINK TO SOURCE

The destruction of forests through logging, mining, extraction of oil and gas, or conversion to agriculture also contributes to the greenhouse effect by releasing carbon into the atmosphere. Such activities have been taking place in the Brazilian rain forest for many years, removing huge amounts of carbon from rain forest ecosystems. Now the same thing is happening in the boreal forest. As transnational resource corporations come under increasing criticism for clear-cut logging and mining in the tropical and temperate rain forests, many of these companies are forced to look elsewhere for timber, petroleum, and other resources. Canada's boreal forest has long been ripe for the plucking. But the situation is much graver in Russia, with its vast resources of high-quality coniferous softwoods and plentiful oil, gas, and mineral reserves —many of which can be found in or near boreal forest ecosystems.

Despite Russia's crippling bureaucracy and widespread corruption, these resources have continued to attract international investment and multiple joint ventures.

*The destruction of forests through logging, mining,
extraction of oil and gas, or conversion to agriculture
also contributes to the greenhouse effect by releasing carbon
into the atmosphere.*

In addition to shaving the landscape of its forests, clear-cut logging releases huge amounts of carbon into the atmosphere while reducing the ability of the ravaged ecosystem to store carbon. At the northern margins, where the tree line meets permafrost, the logging of boreal forests releases methane gas, which has a warming effect twenty times as potent as that of carbon dioxide. Under normal conditions, permafrost—frozen ground that stores the moisture that forests depend on—melts in the summer, releasing the water and nutrients to the trees and surrounding vegetation. But mass deforestation exposes permafrost to direct sunlight, causing previously forested ground to turn into swamp. That's what has climatologists so worried about the Russian taiga right now: the wood panel industry has recently turned its sights on Siberian larch, most of which grows in the permafrost area.

In a country the size of Russia, deforestation and the burning of peatlands release large quantities of carbon. In Siberia, which contains 70 percent of the Russian taiga, logging has reached 40,142 square kilometers (15,500 square miles) per year, with some 10,360 square kilometers (4000 square miles) eliminated by forest fires annually.

From all available evidence, it is clear that natural disturbances are combining with timber extraction to turn the boreal forest from a net sink, or absorber, of carbon *from* the atmosphere to a temporary net source of carbon *to* the atmosphere, further augmenting the greenhouse effect. "Up until about 1970, it looked like the forests were taking up more than half again of [the carbon] we are actually emitting," ecologist Michael J. Apps told a Canadian Senate subcommittee hearing on the Canadian boreal forests in 1997. But all that had changed: in the last five years, forests had begun to lose carbon. "Just looking at the effect of disturbances on the way carbon is stored in the forest," Apps went on, "taking into account fire, insects and harvesting, and keeping track of the carbon that we remove by harvesting and putting it into wood products ... we were a sink and now we have become a bit of a source."

The Effects of Global Warming

The gradual attrition of boreal forests through climate change is part of an ecological domino effect that's happening all over the world. In the tropics, a huge portion of the planet's coral reefs—which take thousands of years to grow and which act as natural breakwaters to prevent beaches from washing away—is dead or dying. Endless kilometers of reefs from the Indian Ocean to the western Pacific have either disappeared or died because of the loss of algae due to climate warming. (Studies show that temperature rises of only 1°c [1.8°F] can kill a reef in just over two months—one month with a rise of 2°c [3.6°F].)

In some parts of the Pacific Northwest, climate change is already converting interior forests of Ponderosa pine, Douglas-fir, and other conifers into dry grassland and shrubby woodlands. It is now believed that the total area of forest in this region is likely to shrink as grasslands migrate northward. In Washington State's Mount Rainier National Park—famous for its summer wildflower displays—there may soon be nothing left of the flowers if the decay of surrounding forest ecosystems, pumped by the forces of natural disturbance, continues at the current rate. In the Oregon Cascades region, a warming of 2.5°c (4.5°F) would probably allow sagebrush to replace broad expanses of forest, including most of the western hemlock forests.

One of the most influential recent studies of global warming in the boreal forest is the Mackenzie Basin Impact Study (1997). This six-year project, sponsored by Environment Canada, was designed to estimate future climate conditions of the Mackenzie Basin, a boreal watershed of 1.7 million square kilometers (0.66 million square miles) in the Canadian Northwest Territories. According to the study, the Mackenzie Basin warmed an average of 1.7°C (3.1°F) over the previous one hundred years—three times the global rate of 0.3° to 0.6°C (0.5° to 1.1°F). This warming has led to historically low water levels in Great Slave Lake—the deepest lake in North America. Permafrost melting, erosion, and landslides have also increased as a result of record forest fires in the region. The five worst forest fire seasons on record had all occurred since 1980. Of the 7 million hectares (17 million acres) of boreal forest across Canada that went up in smoke in 1995, almost 4 million hectares (almost 10 million acres) was in the Northwest Territories and Yukon.

Forecasting the future climate of the Mackenzie Basin under a doubling of carbon dioxide concentrations, University of British Columbia ecologist Stewart J. Cohen and his colleagues projected that warming will continue to lower the water levels and melt permafrost, causing an increase in landslides. The annual area of forest burned will double, coniferous trees will die as a result of drought, and trees such as the white pine will be more susceptible to insects. Wildlife species more dependent on old-growth forests—such as the marten, fisher, and caribou—will be forced by these developments to move northward, where a more sparse forest ecosystem will threaten their survival.

Dr. Jim Bruce of the Intergovernmental Panel on Climate Change sees the Mackenzie Basin test results as an ominous precedent by which the entire boreal region can be measured. "What we've seen here in the Mackenzie over the past two decades," said

Bruce, speaking at a climate change workshop held in Yellow-knife in May 1996, "is part of the climate signal: a foretaste of what's to come. Lower lake/river levels, more sediment from landslides, permafrost melting. It's the beginning of a process."

Another research project for the Arctic region showed that ice extent (the area within the ice-ocean margin) and ice area (the area of ice-covered ocean) decreased 4.5 percent from 1978 to 1987 and 5.6 percent from 1987 to 1994. The indigenous Inuvialuit people living in Tuktoyaktuk, Northwest Territories, reported higher wave action and increased erosion. Simply put, the ice cover had become less compact over the period and showed signs of break-ing up—the first time in history such a trend had been established.

Another study, by researchers Allen Solomon and Rik Lee-mans, compared boreal forest responses to environmental change during the past twenty thousand years (the Last Glacial Maxi-mum) with projected responses for the next two hundred years. As well as determining the role of climate change in disrupting the boreal ecosystem, this research was a useful way of predicting global terrestrial carbon cycling and estimating future wood sup-plies. Using both the present climate and that of the Last Glacial Maximum, Solomon and Leemans developed predictions of veg-etation distribution under a possible climate scenario two hun-dred years in the future. The study was based on a scenario in which atmospheric carbon dioxide levels were doubled from the present rate.

Although the global area of boreal aquatic biomass today is almost 2½ times greater than during the Last Glacial Maximum, the scenarios for future climates suggest that the total potential area in which boreal forests would be able to grow would be between 14 and 42 percent less than their extent today.

LONG-RANGE FORECAST

According to University of Alberta aquatic ecologist David Schindler, the science of how carbon dioxide and other gases warm the atmosphere is now "100 percent agreed upon." There is, to be sure, continuing skepticism surrounding the countervailing effects of sulfur oxides, cloud cover, and other hard-to-predict factors such as carbon dioxide fertilization, a "feedback" of carbon dioxide that some scientists believe enhances the growth of trees unless other factors limit the trees' absorption of carbon dioxide. What is less debatable, Schindler wrote in 1998, is that even mild greenhouse warming will have catastrophic environmental effects. And surely these effects are more important than the economic ones.

According to the IPCC, if the present rate of fossil fuel emissions continues, the next century will see an increase in greenhouse gases great enough to raise global temperatures by 1.1° to 3.3°C (2° to 6°F). Even if concentrations of greenhouse gases such as carbon dioxide and methane are stabilized by the year 2100, most studies project temperature increases beyond that date. The IPCC's "best guess" is that temperatures over the next few decades may increase fifteen to thirty times faster than ever before, and they will rise to a level that has not been reached in more than 150,000 years. In such a scenario, forests and wildlife in the high-latitude countries of the boreal region—Canada, the Scandinavian countries, Alaska, and Russia—will suffer the most stress.

Evidence is growing that climate, human activity, and the boreal forest are linked in a vicious cycle.

All this would mean, among other things: the loss of plant life and biodiversity throughout the boreal region; the disappearance of animal habitat, causing the loss of between 10 and 50 percent of boreal animal species; the resettlement of entire communities as a result of flooding and forest fires; and the loss or degradation of valuable timber and water resources that feed the South. Scientists have already established that northern latitudes are vulnerable to the effects of global warming. The only question remaining is how pervasive those effects will be. Evidence is growing that climate, human activity, and the boreal forest are linked in a vicious cycle: climate change—both naturally caused and human-influenced—is adversely affecting the forest, whose destruction by industry is, in turn, feeding the forces that cause climate change.

The IPCC is now predicting that two-thirds of the boreal forest will undergo major changes in vegetation and ecosystems in the next century. At the same time, as already mentioned, the average surface temperature over the next century will increase from 1.1° to 3.3°C (2° to 6°F). In its 1996–97 report, the IPCC concluded that increases of as little as 1°C (1.8°F) in mean annual air temperature will be enough to affect the growth and regeneration capacity of many tree species. In several regions, the increased temperature will alter the function and composition of the forests; in others, it will cause forest cover to vanish completely. Much of the boreal forest will be replaced by grasslands, temperate forest, or tundra.

How will these changes occur? Initially, there might be a burst of tree growth in some boreal forests as a result of increased warming. But several studies indicate that such growth is often short-lived.

Here are some of the expected changes across the green halo:

- According to Environment Canada, seedlings that are currently being planted will reach only half of their harvestable age by about year 2030. By that time, they will be growing in a changed climate in which they'll be exposed to a much higher degree of disturbances.
- In western Canada, a series of droughts will increase the prairielike conditions throughout the region, disrupting vegetative growth and reproduction in the south. These conditions—and the migration of southern temperate insects, such as the white pine weevil, to the boreal region—will

cause a net loss in the total area of the western Canadian boreal forest.

- In Atlantic Canada, scientists predict an increase in the number and severity of storms, leading to more large-scale blowdowns of Maritime boreal forests. The younger forests' capacity to serve as a carbon sink will be weakened by stresses such as air pollution—especially acid rain and acid fog.
- In the Siberian taiga—the largest chunk of the world's boreal forest—there is no evidence of change in tree growth rates. But global warming has accelerated the rate of forest fires throughout the country, not only destroying trees and peatland but also forcing many endangered species to the outer limits of the forest, where they will either starve (woodland caribou) or be hunted (Siberian tiger) to extinction. Communities that depend on nearby mines or oil or gas operations will suffer infrastructure damage from melting permafrost.

In Alaska, there's really no need to predict the long-term effects of climate change—they've already begun. According to forest ecologist Glenn Juday, an associate professor of forest ecology at the University of Alaska, Fairbanks, the state of Alaska has become a crystal ball for climate change in the North. The low range of warming predicted for the planet as a whole by the year 2100 has already occurred in the city of Fairbanks, which has seen its average warm-season temperature go up by nearly 1.7°C (3°F) in the last half century. Glaciers have generally receded—in some places they're about 9 meters (30 feet) thinner than forty years ago. In addition to permafrost melting, erosion, landslides, and floods, the growth rate of Alaska's boreal forests has "gone into the tank," as Juday put it in an interview with the *New York Times*.

Except for a brief period of cooling caused by the eruption of

the Mt. Pinatubo volcano in 1991, there has been a continuous
warming in Alaska that hasn't slowed since the late 1970s. And
that warming is having an effect on surrounding ecosystems.
Across much of the central interior of the state—one of the dri-
est regions in Alaska—the reduction in summer rain and the rise
in summer temperature have accelerated the rate of evaporation
while lengthening the growing season in the forest. The combination of these factors—which has led to earlier springs and later
falls—has pushed the moisture supply down to critical levels.

As a result, trees are growing more slowly. Because the winters
are milder, snowfalls are heavier and wetter. Thick blankets of wet
snow snap off branches and break trees in two, allowing populations of wood-boring insects to increase and survive into the
summer. In south-central Alaska, insect outbreaks have killed
most of the mature spruce trees; in the forests north of the Alaska
range, the spruce budworm (previously unknown there) has
defoliated some 23,000 hectares (57,000 acres) of forest. According to Juday, these developments are a direct consequence of a
major climate shift that started more than twenty years ago, and
the effects are beginning to compound each other. "We've certainly experienced some amazing things," he says, with some
understatement.

Ironically, climate change will hurt the industry that contributes to some of these effects on the boreal forest. Multinational
logging companies, in the interests of continuing assured access
to valued resources, will be faced with the increasing financial
burden of fire suppression and other services required to combat
the effects of wildfires, insect infestation, and storm damage.
Over the next few decades, the size of the harvestable forest will
shrink, putting more pressure on the lumber industry to trade
in value-added products. Forest companies can no longer deny
that fossil fuel consumption contributes to climate change,
which, in turn, threatens the forest ecosystem whose trees provide

the industry with its wealth. For self-preservation, if for no other reason, industry must recognize its role in the boreal forest's diminishing resources and respond with practices that will work for all concerned: the forest, its flora and fauna, and the people who depend on its continued good health.

CHAPTER 5

Transnational Corporations: A Rush for the Spoils

The earth, like trees, dies from the top down. The things that are killing the North will kill, if left unchecked, everything else.

—Margaret Atwood, *Strange Things: The Malevolent North in Canadian Literature*

Most scientists now agree that global warming is a reality. There is also general agreement about some of its effects on terrestrial ecosystems such as the boreal forest. But identifying the exact role that industrial activities play in global warming has so far proved elusive, and there is less consensus about the extent of its influence.

It is clear, however, that activities such as logging, mining, and oil exploration have other deleterious effects on the ecosystem. Scientists generally agree that there is too much unregulated industrial activity in the boreal forest. But how much is too much? And why have we allowed it to spin out of control?

Over the last century, logging, mining, and oil exploration in the boreal forests of Russia, North America, and Scandinavia have led to the gradual attrition of these forests. When combined with global warming, these activities threaten to consume the entire green halo in another two hundred years. Since the collapse of the Soviet Union, the Russian taiga has undergone a speculative rush from transnational resource corporations. Much of the original Scandinavian forest has disappeared already; the remainder has been converted to managed tree farms or mixed second-growth forests. In Canada, 65 percent of the boreal forest is locked into long-term logging contracts. And the Alaskan taiga is under threat from all kinds of development. Thanks to these events, the boreal forest is vanishing faster than it can regenerate.

THE FOREST—OURS TO EXPLOIT

Modern forest management originated in 18th-century Germany as a by-product of the Enlightenment. Before then, German policymakers generally held the opinion that the best way to protect forests was to restrict their use. As Swedish historian Anders Ockerman has put it, forests were looked upon as a "mine" of limited resources. But this early conservationist philosophy gradually disappeared as Germany's forests began to dwindle. With no colonies to provide timber reserves, the Germans came up with the principle of sustained yield: the notion that each forest could sacrifice a certain number of trees, according to a cycle that lasted for centuries, and remain a healthy ecosystem. Despite the initial resistance to this concept in 19th-century America—where early conservationists raised disturbing new questions about the effects on wildlife habitat—the philosophy of sustained yield has survived to this day. Indeed, it is the raison d'être of the international timber industry—the proof, apparently, that modern forestry works.

Unfortunately, modern forestry has led to the degradation of ecosystems and biodiversity. Early foresters did not have the knowledge to foresee these consequences. Today, the science of conservation biology attempts to combine sound ecological knowledge with sustainable forestry practice by trying to answer two important questions: How does nature work? And how can human beings coexist with nature?

The main problem is that the mass-consumption goals of capitalism in the last hundred years contradict the principle of sustainability. By the late 19th century, it was becoming obvious that consumerism and conservation were antithetical in purpose. The philosophy of mass consumption tends to view the earth and its resources as completely separate from social and regional realities. "Historically," write F. Stuart Chapin and Gail Whiteman, "for many commercial organizations, the 'environment' was considered a strictly social, political and economic arena, with the earth as an abundant, hidden backdrop." In the context of today's hypercompetitive market environment, concepts such as forest sustainability—which cannot be measured by the year but must be calculated over decades to centuries—tend to get low priority when business decisions are being made.

The philosophy of mass consumption tends to view the earth and its resources as completely separate from social and regional realities.

When conservationists now use the term "sustainable forestry," they're usually referring to the practice of selective logging, by which the overall diversity of a forest can be preserved. Under "sustainable forestry," nature can coexist with development. Unfortunately, high demand for timber has prevented most multinational companies from adopting selective logging for the majority of their operations. These days, the forest industry continues to use the same clear-cutting methods in the taiga that it claims to have abandoned in other forest ecosystems.

Mining and oil exploration may not remove as much forest as the logging industry, but the effect on surrounding ecosystems can be equally devastating when these activities are conducted irresponsibly. Mining and drilling often pollute rivers, lakes, and streams, as well as destroying wildlife habitats and affecting human health. One need only mention the *Exxon Valdez* to be reminded of the far-reaching effects of an oil spill.

One World, One Economy—Or Else

One of the most important geopolitical developments in the final half of the 20th century has been the emergence of a global economy run by transnational corporations. For much of the last quarter century, transnational corporations have exerted tremendous influence on international markets and regulations through foreign direct investment and international trade policy developments such as the Multilateral Agreement on Investment (MAI), the North American Free Trade Agreement (NAFTA), and the World Trade Organization (WTO). Through corporate mergers, the influence of transnational corporations has spread even further, allowing a small concentration of interests to control large amounts of resources in every corner of the planet (a consolidation of power only magnified by the frequent overlap of board members among various companies with complementary interests).

The MAI caused special concern because of the sweeping powers it would have granted transnational corporations while crippling the regulatory powers of nations. The agreement, which was temporarily shelved in early 1998, also contained a number of provisions that would have posed an immediate environmental threat throughout the world. Among other things, it would have allowed profit making by international corporations and investors to override local or federal regulations protecting the environment. It would also have given corporations the power to sue governments enacting regulations that in any way inhibited the ability to make profits. Canadian environmentalists frequently cite a similar provision in NAFTA that allowed the Ethyl Corporation to sue the Canadian government for $251 million for banning the use of a toxic new additive in Canadian gasoline because of its health hazard.

Although an international movement of grassroots opposition in February 1998 helped stall negotiations to enact the MAI, a new attempt is now under way to move the negotiations from the twenty-nine-member Organization for Economic Cooperation and Development (OECD) to the World Trade Organization. As this book went to press, the World Trade Organization was planning to negotiate an agreement that would eliminate all tariffs on forest products throughout the world. Also on the table was a plan to eliminate nontariff forest protection measures such as forest management standards, exotic species regulations, and building codes that protect domestic industry. Conservationists believe that such an agreement (in some quarters referred to as the Global Free Logging Agreement) will lead to increased consumption of global forests, making it even more of a challenge to reform currently unsustainable forestry practices.

Transnational corporations and the global economy they serve are based on an ideology of economic determinism. They are, as the philosopher John Ralston Saul has put it, "the seat of contemporary feudalism." Because they transcend national boundaries and have multiple billions of dollars at their disposal, transnational corporations are like phantoms—they can rarely be touched by individuals or communities. Local populations and their concerns are seen as unfortunate obstacles to the higher goal of maximizing sales at the lowest possible cost. "International economic feudalism is based on the constant ability to shift investments or production from one national area to another in an ongoing auction for more favourable conditions," writes Saul. "The ultimate weapon is the threat to decamp each time there is a discussion of wage levels, job security, health standards, environmental standards or any standards at all relating to place and people."

The international banking system has been crucial to the global economy's development. In the wake of the Soviet Union's collapse, major financial institutions from wealthier countries were more than eager to provide letters of credit and foreign exchange accounts for cash-poor but resource-rich former Communist countries. In 1996, for example, the Export-Import Bank of the United States began offering loan guarantees to Russian companies buying American equipment and services for the pulp, paper, timber, and wood products industries.

The increasing power of transnational corporations, along with a more globalized economy, has made the work of preserving forest ecosystems all the more difficult. As timber, mining, and petroleum interests have gained access to ever-expanding markets, the rate of consumption has increased exponentially. In today's accelerated business climate, the prospect of monitoring the daily activities of transnational resource companies—particularly those operating in more remote regions of the planet—has become all the more daunting.

Because they transcend national boundaries and have multiple billions of dollars at their disposal, transnational corporations are like phantoms—they can rarely be touched by individuals or communities.

Beyond the glare of media scrutiny, international logging, mining, and oil companies are able to extract resources from the forest without being held accountable for the effect on biodiversity, animal habitat, or local human populations. Unlike tropical and temperate rain forests, where clear-cut logging has been widely condemned by the international community in recent years, boreal forests are far enough removed from major media centers or tourist meccas to prevent widespread public awareness of industrial activity. In some cases, it is only through the Internet—from reports by field scientists or NGOs and their environmental researchers—that industrial abuses of the boreal forests ever come to light.

The Boreal Forest: A Barometer of Excess

In December 1998, the Taiga Rescue Network released a joint NGO statement declaring the boreal forest "one of the world's clearest examples of the link between high consumption, late 20th century industrial society and the collapse of natural ecosystems." Government incentives such as tax breaks and low concession and stumpage fees have given transnational corporations free rein in the boreal forest. Deregulation has also allowed illegal activity such as timber and animal poaching and black market trade to flourish in cash-poor countries such as Russia.

At the same time, the local languages, cultural identity, land rights, and traditional lifestyles of indigenous people are gradually disappearing. In the West, land use policy is too often determined by government and industry without consultation with local or aboriginal populations. In North America, this top-down approach often results in decisions that are destructive to indigenous communities. In the former Soviet Union, the privatization of state land has resulted in short-term exploitation by new owners, many of whom are fly-by-night profiteers with no previous experience in forest management.

"The enormous financial and political power of the largest companies adds dramatically to pressures on ecosystems that had previously been too remote to attract attention," the joint NGO statement reads. "The tiny human population of the [boreal forest] means that many of the arguments used to explain away forest loss elsewhere—'overpopulation,' food production, firewood collection and recreation—simply do not apply. Stripped of excuses, the central role played by global industry becomes obvious."

The biggest threat to the taiga today is exploding timber demand. According to the U.S.-based Center for International Trade in Forest Products (CINTRAFOR), that situation is about to get worse. By the year 2025, China could face an annual deficit in industrial wood of some 200 million cubic meters (260 million cubic yards). (Japan, the world leader, currently imports about 80 million cubic metres [105 million cubic yards].) It doesn't take an economics expert to guess where the People's Republic will turn for its imported timber. "Outside of Siberia and the Russian Far

East," a 1996 CINTRAFOR report concludes, "very few regions have the ability to service this looming deficit."

How Russia will withstand the inevitable assault on its resources is anybody's guess. But if boreal forests across the green halo are ever to improve their long-term survival prospects, the old maxim of "think globally, act locally" can no longer be sufficient. Larger issues such as mass consumption, increased demand for timber, and the dominance of global capital have moved the debate on forests into a completely different realm. As the next few chapters will show, clear-cut logging, mining, and oil exploration are happening far too fast and across far too many economic, political, and national boundaries to be dealt with only on a local basis.

Some scientists and eco-activists have already formed international networks to distribute information about key trade agreements affecting forest ecosystems. And more people are holding governments accountable for giving away their regulatory powers over forest use. But these efforts are only a beginning.

CHAPTER 6

The Russian Taiga: Boreal Mayhem

In the free-for-all that filled the post-Soviet vacuum, Russia's riches are being plundered without thought for the future or care for the land . . . The rush to defile the Motherland is on.

—Andrew Meier, "Cursed Cornucopia," *Time*, December 29, 1997

Trying to come to grips with what is happening in the Russian boreal forest is like trying to cram twenty subjects into a Ph.D. thesis. The Russian Federation is so huge, and its forests so predominant, that it's difficult to arrive at a single conclusion when there are so many conflicting factors of politics, economy, and history crossing so many regional boundaries—each containing its own cultural and environmental distinctions.

What can be said with certainty is that the Russian taiga is now logged, mined, and drilled beyond its capacity to regenerate. The destruction of these forests has ominous implications not only for surrounding communities but also for the global atmosphere—as the biggest piece of the boreal pie, Russia's taiga is one of the world's major sources of terrestrial carbon.

Much of Russia's out-of-control development during the 1990s can be attributed to the pressures of an ailing economy following the collapse of the Soviet Union. The Russian government, strapped for cash, was eager to capitalize on the country's natural resources. Selling them off to foreign interests was the quickest and easiest way to generate revenue. But a much longer tradition of large-scale development—a product of the Soviet philosophy of "giantism"—continues to haunt Russia. The only difference now, in the era of global capitalism, is that the regulatory structure that once governed Russian forests no longer exists, leaving the forests vulnerable not only to foreign control but also to internal corruption and black market crime. Although efforts are being made to preserve more of the forest as parkland, Russian scientists are worried that the problems of regulation, foreign ownership, and corruption are not being addressed quickly enough to stem the tide of destruction.

Soviet Giantism: A Taiga Legacy

The Russian federation contains the largest forest area of any nation in the world—an estimated 750 million to 771 million hectares (1850 million to 1900 million acres) stretching from the Ural Mountains in the west to the Pacific Ocean in the east. This mass of trees constitutes 60 percent of the world's boreal forests, 54 percent of all coniferous forests, and 21 percent of all remaining standing forests.

It's no surprise that the boreal forest is mythologized in Russian literature. In Boris Pasternak's classic novel *Doctor Zhivago*, the giant taiga forests of Siberia are central to the narrative—a dark metaphor of a great country's struggle on the brink of revolution. Pasternak attributed to the taiga an all-consuming power, a potency far more enduring in its "truth" than the ideological battles being fought on its margins.

At times, the great taiga appears to envelop the characters, if not overwhelm them. When Yuri arrives at a new camp with a convoy of partisan families, he is impressed by the dense, impenetrable forest surrounding the camp beyond the highway. He is convinced he could easily get lost in it. The edge of the taiga also serves as the front line:

There was fighting on the western edges of the *tayga*. But

the *tayga* was so immense that the battles were like border warfare on the edges of its kingdom, and the camp, hidden within its heart, so full of people that however many went away to fight, there seemed always to be more left.

It was this sense of endless forest, perhaps, that allowed Russian legislators to be so cavalier about its importance; there were so many trees on this land that the forests would surely last forever. But under the Soviet system, the taiga—like much of the Russian environment during the seventy-year Communist era—became a casualty of central planning. A spirit of "giantism" took over, a dedication to grand-scale development that superseded more sentimental concerns about the environment. Forest protection became the preserve of bourgeois romantics.

Giantism was the aesthetic embodiment of Stalin's edifice complex. Everything had to be designed on a garishly grand scale to glorify the Revolution: gigantic buildings and bridges, towering monuments to Soviet heroes, and so on. The larger-than-life scenes depicted in social realist paintings implied that monolithic infrastructure was the only route to prosperity and a sign of progress only the proletarian collective could achieve. These grandiose experiments continued well after Stalin's death. Hydroelectric dams, especially, symbolized Russian might in the same manner as troops and rockets. As one writer put it, they embodied "man's conquest over nature and [were] the article of Communist faith." Of course, the dams also flooded millions of hectares of forests, displaced entire indigenous communities, and destroyed fishing grounds.

Columbia University humanities professor Simon Schama captured the essence of giantism and its impact on forests in his far-ranging study of culture and environment, *Landscape and Memory*. In one passage, Schama explains why Soviet border guards once cleared a strip of forest 12 meters (40 feet) wide along the Byelorussian and Polish border using a huge, growling machine known as Big Mower:

> For the Soviet state, like many of its predecessors, forestry
> was a branch of state security ... For the woods had a way of
> invading the routemap of the police state with their under-
> growth, creating botanically sheltered places of sedition. No
> doubt about it, the woods were reactionary accomplices in
> the chauvinist conspiracy to undermine People's Democracy.

This mentality was evident in Stalin's treatment of the Trans-Siberian Railway project. The railway, which today spans more than 9000 kilometers (5600 miles) from Moscow to Vladivostok, was constructed to accelerate the pace of colonization, protect Russia's southern borders and eastern shores from China and Japan, and develop large industrial centers along the railway to extract raw materials for domestic use and export. But under the Soviet system, industry fell under state control and Moscow developed the Far East as a prime resource from which to extract oil and gas, timber, fish, gold, and diamonds.

During the Stalin era, entire cities were constructed with names such as Uglegorsk (coal town) and Neftegorsk (oil town), each focusing on one or two resources. At the same time, much of the countryside was converted into slave labor camps—the infamous gulag archipelago described in Aleksandr Solzhenitsyn's best-selling 1974 book of the same name. The intent of these camps, established throughout Siberia and the Far East in places such as Khabarovsk, Vladivostok, Sakhalin, Kamchatka, and the gold-rich Kolyma River basin, was supposedly to serve the mass industrialization of Russia. But at their peak in the 1930s, they held more than 21 million prisoners and had an annual death rate of 25 percent. In one of the 20th century's sadder ironies, the forests surrounding these massive graveyards—where millions of people lost their lives in the name of Communist revolutionary progress—are now some of the most heavily exploited free-enterprise zones for foreign-based interests.

The subject of giantism was foremost in my thoughts when I met Russian ecologist Andrei Laletin during my visit to Estonia in fall 1998. Laletin, the epitome of the Russian lab scientist with his flowing black beard, thick, rolling accent, and Coke-bottle glasses, was attending the 4th Taiga Rescue Network conference on behalf of the World Conservation Union. Also known as the International Union for Conservation of Nature and Natural Resources, or IUCN, it's one of the leading monitors of biodiversity protection in the world. A passionate conservationist, Laletin has dedicated his life to saving the Russian boreal forest, and he spent the better part of an afternoon talking with me. As he tells it, the spirit of giantism dies hard in the post-Communist era, haunting Russia's forests to this day.

"Everything was supposed to be huge because it was a very easy way to steal money," he told me, explaining the Soviet logic of giantism. "For example, to build any channel, you could write that it cost you one million rubles when you spent only one *thousand* rubles." The problem, Laletin laments, was that the state never considered the ecological consequences of such an approach: big development, uninhibited by limits or regulations, usually meant that large pieces of landscape, including forests, were sacrificed to build a socialist utopia.

Sadly, the capitalist mentality that replaced this vision has turned out to be no less of a menace for the forest. The only difference is that—rather than being sacrificed on the altar of Soviet glory—the Russian taiga is being cleared for the lustier goal of maximizing short-term profits. In Siberia, the legacy of giantism can be seen in at least three industrial developments Laletin is currently fighting.

In the first case, he says, the World Conservation Union recently announced that rocket fuel contamination has become one of the top threats to the Siberian forest. Partly a legacy of the Soviet space program, the toxic contamination caused by rocket fuel—especially in the remote wilderness area along the borders of Altai, Khakasia, and Tuva—is more recently the by-product of commercial satellite launches.

When rockets are launched in the neighboring republic of Kazakstan, the boosters that propel the rockets into their final orbit fall back to Earth, where they are programmed by the Russian Space Agency to land in Siberia. Rocket fuel often contains heptyl, a substance more toxic than most chemical weapons. Fallen rocket boosters have been known to ignite heptyl-induced fires, contaminate soil, and sometimes poison villages. During the Soviet era, when missile tests and rocket launches were top secret, most of the Russian people did not realize what was happening to the environment—or to their bodies. "People didn't know why they had problems with their health," explains Laletin. "Why their children were born yellow, why there is a lot of cancer in some regions, or why trees get yellow needles."

In a second case Laletin tells me about, a hydroelectric power station in the Boguchany district has destroyed several square kilometers of boreal forest surrounding the Angara River, forcing twenty thousand people from their traditional homelands. Construction of the Boguchany Dam, located near Krasnoyarsk, was begun in the early 1970s with the intention of supplying hydroelectric energy to nearby Japan. But the project is not yet finished, and the government has spent millions of American dollars on it. (In 1997, President Boris Yeltsin and Japanese prime minister Hashimoto announced their support for a renewed effort to complete the dam.) Russia's support of the project is based on the potential revenue represented by the sale of hydroelectric power. But the project has forced the people of Angara River to pack up and leave, despite having spent generations living in harmony with the forest: picking mushrooms, berries, and nuts; making honey; running small agricultural gardens. Before the dam project uprooted them, the people were self-sufficient. Now the dam will provide the only job opportunities in the area.

In the third case, Laletin's organization, Friends of the Siberian Forest, is fighting a decision by the regional parliament of Krasnoyarsk not to hold a referendum on building a second nuclear power plant near the city. Following the Chernobyl disaster of 1986, the Kremlin was forced to lift the veil of secrecy surrounding the existence of so-called nuclear cities in the Soviet Union. One of these places was Chelyabinsk, a small city near Krasnoyarsk. For years, plutonium was produced and uranium enriched at a nuclear plant in the area. Now, the government wants to build a second processing plant—even importing nuclear waste from Chernobyl and other nuclear power stations to support it. Aside from making no ecological sense, the idea breaks Russian law: it's illegal to import nuclear waste from another country, as Ukraine is now.

These are just a few of the problems facing the boreal forest in a single region of Russia. Although their effect on surrounding forests is serious enough, they don't begin to approach the scale of destruction achieved by the logging, petroleum, or mining industries.

OIL AND GAS EXPLORATION: BLEEDING THE EARTH DRY

In many parts of the boreal forest, the oil and gas industry does more damage than logging. As well as removing large tracts of forest, petroleum exploration pollutes streams and—when leakage or spills occur—contaminates surrounding ecosystems. Before drilling even begins, oil and gas companies use clear-cut logging to open up potential sites for exploration.

Access roads and seismic lines chew up even more forest. Seismic lines are long, narrow pathways cut through the forest to conduct seismic soundings that allow geophysicists to find out what's underground. Often used by oil companies to locate oil or gas reserves, seismic lines tend to be about 5 to 7 meters (16 to 23 feet) wide and anywhere from half a kilometer to hundreds of kilometers long. When viewed from above, they make the forest look like a giant chessboard. Many seismic lines contain dozens to hundreds of holes, sunk at regular intervals to a depth of about 20 meters (65 feet), where dynamite blasts are used to open underground reservoirs. (More recently, seismic work is being done with vibrating machines without producing holes.) Regardless of the method, seismic lines tear up the forest and threaten wildlife by providing quick and easy access for poachers. In Russia, the poachers include members of the oil and gas industry, who use company equipment, including helicopters and all-terrain vehicles, to hunt animals for sport and food.

In Russian old-growth forests, the frequency of fires has increased two to three times in recent decades because of the industry's presence.

In Russia, the oil and gas industry's destructive impact on the boreal forest has had a snowball effect, combining fires and industrial accident. In Russian old-growth forests, the frequency of fires has increased two to three times in recent decades because of the industry's presence. In some parts of Russia, such as the Khanty-Mansiysk region, it's not unusual for as many as a thousand oil spills to occur every year. In fall 1994, an oil spill of between 70,000 and 80,000 tonnes occurred in the Komi area of European Russia. The operation, run by the Komy Arctic Oil Company of Russia, was a joint venture with Gulf Canada and British Gas—corporations that had promised to protect the Russian environment when they negotiated the contracts to develop Russian oil fields.

Russia is a major target because it boasts 36 percent of the world's natural gas reserves and 13 percent of its oil. With 90 billion barrels of known oil reserves, from the Komi Republic in the Northwest to the Yamal Peninsula in western Siberia and Sakhalin Island in the Far East, Russia exports two million barrels a day. Nearly half of Russia's hard currency revenue is generated by oil and gas exports, and oil and gas provide the largest source of income to the Russian state. The average salary in the oil industry is three times as high as in most other sectors of the Russian economy. Loyalty to the industry is strong. Despite a recent downturn in production, oil profits continue to maintain local infrastructures, the social welfare system, medical services, and housing standards. New cities have sprung up in formerly unpopulated taiga areas, and communication systems are cropping up everywhere. So any critique of the industry has to take these factors into account.

By the mid-1990s, new oil and gas development projects were expected to lead to investments of more than U.S.$120 billion over the next two decades. Japan's Itochu Corporation was one of the first out of the starting gate in December 1994, announcing a full-scale development project for crude oil in western Siberia with American and Russian partners. The company, encouraged by the Russian government's decision to waive oil export taxes on the output from the project, set a 1998 target of 25,000 barrels a day (a substantial increase from its production of 6000 barrels per day at the time).

In 1997, two of Russia's energy conglomerates formed alliances with Western companies to jumpstart the country's debt-ridden energy sector to the tune of nearly U.S.$4 billion. Royal Dutch/ Shell alone teed up U.S.$1 billion to develop the company's Siberian deposits. Priming the pump, as it were, was a new commission on natural resources announced by President Boris Yeltsin. Production-sharing agreements would allow foreign firms to export part of the output from any mine or oil field.

The Russian Far East has some of the largest untapped oil and natural gas reserves in the world. From 1992 to 1996, production had declined because there were not enough pipelines. But a few new pipelines solved that problem. By early 1999, a consortium of Russian, Japanese, Chinese, and British investors was planning to build a 2000-kilometer (1240-mile) gas and oil pipeline to serve Chinese and Korean markets. The pipeline would connect the Kovykta gas fields of Irkutsk to the Pacific Ocean by cutting through the forests and the steppes of the Irkutsk and Buriatia regions near Lake Baikal, continuing through Mongolia and northern China.

The government is also building shelf reserves off Sakhalin, Magadan, Kamchatka, and Khabarovsk in the Far East. The huge Sakhalin oil projects are furthest ahead: the Sakhalin Energy Investment Company—a consortium of Shell, Mitsubishi, Mitsui, MacDermott, and Marathon—is planning to pump U.S.$30 billion into four offshore projects.

The Sakhalin development is expected to have a major effect on the surrounding environment. The drilling area is a fragile ecosystem, subject to occasional seismic activity and tidal waves. The region's ice cliffs and pack ice are vulnerable to such disturbances, and the possible collapse into icebergs could knock out a pipeline or two. If an earthquake or a tidal wave were to hit an area close to a petroleum development, the resulting damage to local flora caused by leakage and spills would be considerable. In 1995, Exxon postponed drilling in the northern Sakhalin community of Neftegorsk because of a massive earthquake that killed 60 percent of the town's 3200 residents.

Siberia is another hot spot of oil exploration in the boreal forest. About 80 percent of Russian oil and gas reserves are located in the central and northern areas of western Siberia. During the late 1960s, oil was discovered in the basin of the Ob River. The Soviet government immediately began exploring the region and by the early 1980s had established a major petroleum area called Samotlor, near Nizhnevartovsk. An American research team visiting the area filed this chilling report of environmental conditions in the region:

Today throughout the area, oil spills and casual pollution blacken the wetlands, raised roads trap water causing flooding and ruining the forests, fires caused by oil worker carelessness and petroleum-soaked debris send columns of smoke into the air, and acid rain blights huge territories. Western Siberia, like the American Appalachian coal fields at the beginning of this century, has become a national sacrifice area.

Now, in the same region, a proposed park that would protect the land of more than eight hundred Khanty people is being subverted by the Russian government and oil companies, despite support from the local populations. This dismissal of local concerns is nothing new. In northwestern Siberia, the traditional homelands of at least seven indigenous tribes have been ruined or severely compromised by oil and gas activity. Many aboriginal families can no longer herd reindeer because all the pastures are gone. Even those willing to lend their land to oil companies are often poorly compensated. One family that lent its land to the American oil company Amoco was given a walkie-talkie, a generator, eight sacks of flour, sugar, tea, and eight batteries as compensation.

MINING: THE HIDDEN FACTOR

Inside a tunnel that leads to the Norilsk copper factory in northern Russia, visitors are greeted by a scrawled message that reads: "Welcome to hell." It's a fitting introduction to Norilsk, located above the Arctic Circle, about 3500 kilometers (2200 miles) from Moscow. Built in the 1930s by political prisoners, this frozen wasteland is the bleakest of industrial outposts—an ecological disaster zone worse than what any science fiction writer could invent. Wedged between mountains of ore, it lies beneath a sulfur dioxide haze. From above, only towering smokestacks can be seen. All the larch forests surrounding Norilsk are dead. In total, air pollution has killed some 4000 square kilometers (1540 square miles) of boreal forest. Among the people of Norilsk, tuberculosis runs rampant.

According to *Time* magazine, Norilsk is the Russian republic's "most prodigious producer of precious metals." It provides nearly all of the country's platinum and palladium (between 25 and 50 percent of the world's platinum originates in Norilsk), and most of Russia's copper, nickel, and cobalt. Not surprisingly, the smelters of Norilsk are the world's single largest air polluter, emitting some 2.3 million metric tonnes of sulfur dioxide every year.

Norilsk is only the most extreme example in Russia of the destructive effect that mining can have on a boreal forest. Across Russia, industrial emissions from mining alone have killed at least 1 million hectares (2.5 million acres) of forest. It's difficult to trace the full ecological impact of mining because most of the activity takes place underground. One of the most damaging effects is the use of toxic metals in processing. In the boreal regions of Russia, the gold-mining industry is one of the main causes of mercury poisoning. Using mercury to separate gold is now illegal, but many small gold-mining operations still use it—thus contributing to the toxic poisoning of freshwater streams and fish. But some scientists consider cyanide leaching no less dangerous to the ecosystem. Government regulators had a new problem on their hands when construction of a gold mine using this method—the first in the Russian republic—began in 1998.

In the Amur Oblast, nearly 18,000 hectares (44,000 acres) of forest have been stripped by gold mining, and salmon rivers have been poisoned. An estimated 1500 rivers and streams have also been polluted in the Magadan region, and the geochemical balance of the Kolyma River basin has undergone major changes as a result of gold mining. Concentrations of liquid waste saturate the earth around gold extraction plants such as the Metrasova plant in the Omchak valley. In the Komi Republic, gold mining is taking place in the Yugyd Va National Nature Park, in the basin of the Kozhim River, which is included on the UNESCO World Natural Heritage List, an international index of protected areas. Gold mining has also devastated old-growth birch forests in Amur.

Gold-mining companies have even managed to penetrate the highlands of Tuva, one of Russia's most isolated republics. Nearly two days' drive from the Trans-Siberian Railroad, Tuva is several mountain passes away from the developed world. The indigenous peoples in Tuva still travel only on horseback and manage their natural resources according to shamanistic and Buddhist traditions. Northeastern Tuva contains one of Russia's largest areas of unroaded forest, with 4 million hectares (10 million acres) of taiga, including Siberian pine, fir, spruce, and larch. But now Tuva's Bii-Kem River watershed, also known as the Upper Yenisey, is being threatened by a proposed gold mine that will open new roads and expose the area to illegal hunting and illegal logging.

The mining projects jeopardizing biodiversity, animal habitat, and indigenous populations in Russia are too numerous to list here, but one thing they have in common is committed foreign investment; from 1996 to 1998, mining in Russia increased by 20 percent. In the Parapolsky Dol, a wetland area on the Kamchatka Peninsula that borders a state nature reserve, a group of Canadian investors has lobbied hard to obtain a fifteen-year mining license to extract gold. The dol, which provides one of the largest habitats for ducks and geese in northeast Asia, is said to contain gold reserves with an estimated value of U.S.$1.5 billion.

Also in Kamchatka, Far East Gold of Toronto has signed agreements to develop three deposits in Khabarovsk Krai and four in Magadan Oblast, in addition to its operation in the Ametistovoye deposit. Other foreign companies are involved in joint ventures with Russian partners.

The importance of gold mining to the revival of the Russian economy has divided environmentalists and local people. In many regions, the local population supports mining developments because employment opportunities are otherwise nonexistent. But often when foreign companies are present, most of the profits leave the area.

In regions with indigenous populations, mining can threaten the very existence of a culture. In the Murmansk Oblast, for example, the indigenous Sámi population is fighting a mining development that would allow a Russian joint venture to prospect 420 square kilometers (162 square miles) of land until the year 2023. The land in question is a permanent pasture for three of the people's main reindeer herds. According to the most recent census, only about 1730 ethnic Sámi are left in all of Russia. Sámi supporters believe that prospecting and other mining activities will result in the disappearance of reindeer herding, which could then lead to the extinction of the Sámi nation in that area.

RUSSIAN TIMBER: RAW LOGS AND ILLEGAL TRADE

During the Communist era, timber extraction in Russia focused on meeting production quotas. Little attention was given to improving efficiency and logging techniques. From the 1950s onward, the government emphasized production while planting rates lagged far behind the rate of cutting. Meanwhile, plantation survival rates remained low. From 1966 to 1988, Siberia experienced a 10 to 20 percent reduction in the number of new trees.

Since the collapse of the Soviet Union, a new problem has arrived with the dramatic increase in the export of raw logs. According to Russia's Institute for Economic Research, at least 20 percent of all trade in timber is illegal and unreported. Much of the timber leaving the country is unprocessed, and many of those raw logs end up in Japan, China, and South Korea. Most of those logs come from the taiga of the Russian Far East—a region considered a boreal hot spot of industrial activity.

Covering one-third of Russia and an area more than two-thirds the size of the United States, the Far East has in recent years become a Promised Land for the timber industry. Forests cover about 45 percent of the Russian Far East landscape—seven times the entire land mass of Japan. The dominant tree species is larch, which provides 62 percent of the region's timber harvest. The exact figure of uncut forest is unknown, but scientific estimates place it somewhere between 25 and 50 percent. (The central and southern regions are dominated by spruce, Korean pine, fir, and Siberian pine forests.) In Yakutia, a part of the region more than twice the size of Alaska, some forests and mountain ranges are believed to have never seen the imprint of a human foot. In such a remote region—far removed from meddling ecotourists and nosy forest bureaucrats—the logging industry has operated with impunity. According to the Ministry of Foreign Economic Relations, more than one hundred unlicensed timber companies were selling lumber abroad from the Russian Far East region of Primorskiy Krai during the mid-1990s. Illegal timber is often sold overseas at prices well below market value. Some estimates for the year 1994 claimed that more than 30 percent of all timber exports were sold at severely depressed prices.

According to Anatoly Lebedev, a journalist and NGO activist from Primorskiy, the regulatory environment governing Russian forests is in such chaos that it may be a waste of time for conservationists to focus their campaign efforts on illegal logging practices. "Sometimes, because of our legislative mess in Russia, regulations are more destructive than logging practices," Lebedev told me. "So, to be illegal sometimes may be better than legal." In the northwestern European region of Karelia, most logging is legal but destructive because large foreign companies get better access to the forest than smaller, local operators. Lebedev recalled reading one Karelian report on illegal logging practices that cited twenty-five types of illegality committed by local forest service representatives, forest users, loggers, and consumers.

Traditionally, the biggest problem with illegal logging has been the lack of border control. With no checks, it's often impossible to determine where illegally logged timber has come from. "The current practice adopted by regional administrations is to produce one universal document which will include data from the logging site until the export site," says Lebedev. "That was very important, because usually illegally logged timber you could resell to the exporter and the exporter had no idea where the timber was from."

Other factors in the depletion of taiga forests by the logging industry are new road-building projects and the high degree of waste during the timber production process. Faced with the growing scarcity of accessible stands in certain parts of the vast Russian forest, timber companies are building more roads into the wilderness to find new sources of wood. The Sikhote-Alin mountain range and the coast along the Sea of Japan, which contains some of the richest forests in the Russian Far East, are the latest targets. At the same time, between 40 and 60 percent of all timber cut in the Far East is lost in the production process, a figure four times as high as in developed countries. This loss is largely due to the continued use of outdated forestry equipment to cut costs. The Russian forest industry needs to develop more ecologically sound equipment. But so far, foreign firms are only providing the kind of harvesting equipment that allows industry to log faster and in sensitive areas, including steep slopes.

Once an area teeming with wild reindeer, grizzly bears, tigers, and leopards, the Russian Far East is now more famous for its dwindling population of Siberian tigers, the largest member of the cat family.

One effect of all this logging has been an increase in the number of mammal and bird species on the endangered list. Once an area teeming with wild reindeer, grizzly bears, tigers, and leopards, the Russian Far East is now more famous for its dwindling population of Siberian tigers, the largest member of the cat family. Only 250 of these beasts remain. Other endangered species in this region include the Himalayan black bear, lynx, horned mountain goat, Blackiston's fish owl, yellow-throated marten, and Far Eastern forest cat. The burgeoning black market in the wake of Communism's collapse has also devastated these animal populations. Black market trade in the Far East has targeted species from the Amur tiger to protected flora such as Korean pine, ginseng, and black fir. An estimated 70 percent of endangered-species trade to Europe passes through Central Asia, including parts of southern Siberia and the Russian Far East.

Taiga for Sale

Logging in the Russian boreal forest has been accelerated by global trade initiatives. The increase in raw log exports, for example, is partly due to a shift toward joint ventures. In June 1995, the U.S.-based Global Forestry Management Group (GFMG) established the first large-scale American logging joint venture in the Russian Far East. Within a short time, the GFMG began exporting raw logs to Japan. Most joint ventures and foreign capital investment agreements don't involve finished wood products such as building parts or furniture because timber companies are more interested in the short-term gain that log exports provide. One joint venture currently under way between Russia, the United States, and Norway may end up exporting approximately 27.5 million cubic meters (or about 5.5 billion board feet) of timber per year—nearly equal to the timber harvest on all American national forest lands in 1993.

China and Japan have also been major consumers of Russian boreal forests. That situation isn't likely to change, especially because their demand for paper and lumber is expected to explode over the next two decades. Chinese importers are attracted to the rich forests in southern Siberia that border Mongolia and China. At the same time, China is participating in various nontimber development projects that promise to consume vast quantities of taiga forest.

In 1997, the World Bank initiated the Russian Forestry Pilot Project to provide a total of U.S.$60 million in loans to three regions. One of them, Krasnoyarsk, is seeking U.S.$400 million from American, European, and Japanese banks to fund a series of oil, mining, forestry, and dam-building projects—projects that may never receive a full environmental assessment hearing.

When Boris Yeltsin and Prime Minister Hashimoto met in Krasnoyarsk for a November 1997 summit, the two leaders pledged to finish construction of a dam to supply hydroelectric energy to China. At the same time, China and Japan are financing construction of a massive 2000-kilometer (1240-mile) pipeline to pump gas and oil from the Irkutsk region's Kovykta field through Mongolia and China to the Pacific Ocean. Both projects are expected to consume large portions of surrounding taiga.

The sale of forests to international companies is through an open tender process supported by the government. The 1997 Forest Code passed by the Russian Duma set a precedent by allowing foreign corporations to take out long-term leases on forest land. First out of the gate was the administration of Khabarovsk region, which in December 1997 approved the lease of 305,000 hectares (754,000 acres) of forest land in the Sukpai watershed. The lease, awarded to the Malaysian company Rimbunan Hijau International, will last forty-eight years, with an annual allowable cut of 550,000 cubic meters.

The Sukpai watershed, located in south Khabarovsk, provides habitat for many wildlife species, including the Siberian tiger, and is part of a state-sponsored Territory for Traditional Natural Resource Use for many local indigenous people, primarily the Udege. Representatives from Rimbunan Hijau said the company had met with indigenous groups and offered to invest an additional U.S.$100,000 to buy eleven vehicles for the communities. Some concern was raised by environmental groups, however, that indigenous perspectives were absent from the process.

To make matters worse, members of the tender committee did not ask questions about the history of the company, so there was no information about its record of complying with environmental regulations in other countries. On the contrary, there were disturbing signs in its application for the Sukpai watershed. The company's business plan did not include provisions to protect the diversity of plant and animal life in the forest, but it did include provisions for a new road that would bisect 800,000 hectares (2 million acres) of roadless ancient forests in the Samarga River watershed. Finally, Rimbunan's promise to invest in timber processing would have to wait; the first stage of the project focused primarily on raw logs.

Russian and international environmental groups immediately condemned the lease. Aside from giving a foreign corporation complete control over the forests, such agreements appeared to reduce the new Forest Code to a rubber stamp for industrial activity. Representatives from the Khabarovsk Regional Forest Service spoke of the necessity of "developing" the forest, because 220,000 hectares (544,000 acres) of the land were considered "mature and overmature." With that philosophy in the Federal Forest Service, it was no wonder the Malaysian company was also showing interest in the neighboring taiga of Primorskiy Krai; if those forests were tendered with such lip service paid to biodiversity, Rimbunan Hijau would have carte blanche to harvest well over 1 million cubic meters of Russian timber annually until the year 2046.

Rimbunan Hijau was not the only company interested in the Sukpai lease. Taiga Lumber of Canada and the American ITT Rayonier were also early bidders. Now that a precedent has been set, other companies have been lining up for similar deals. This practice raises a disturbing question for scientific and conservationist circles alike: if regional authorities are willing to hand over pieces of forest and the federal government fails to conduct environmental assessments of each lease, how can Russia be expected to uphold its international obligation to promote sustainable forest management?

As a result of this fight for the spoils in the Russian taiga, forest protection has not been a very high priority. In 1993, the Federal Forest Legislation failed to clarify property rights issues and left the door wide open for timber companies to lease forest land for logging and other activities. Despite the implications of this policy, there were no means for the public to participate in the process or oversee the results of land use management decisions. In 1994, Roslesprom—the state-controlled holding company responsible for government shareholdings in the forest sector— released a ten-year forestry development plan that called for more than doubling 1994 logging rates within European Russia. This initiative was not good news for the few remaining undisturbed forests in the area.

In southern Siberia, six new reserves and three new national parks have been created since 1990. This development is a higher rate of wilderness establishment than elsewhere in Russia, but some ecologists believe it's a smoke-screen. The reserves won't protect the most critical ecosystems within the region because forest service agencies and other local government bodies are making it difficult to obtain protected area status for the larger forest areas. As of 1998, the administrative regions of Omsk, Novosibirsk, Altai, and Tomsk still didn't have a single federal-level nature reserve or national park.

Bureaucratic Inertia and the New "Kleptocracy"

In many ways, the current state of the boreal forest in Russia is a result of the country's awkward transition to a free-market economy. During the Soviet era, forest management was run by the state and divided into two functions: the Federal Forest Service, which owned the forests and was responsible for commercial management, documentation, and the granting of logging licenses; and the forest industry, a separate state bureaucracy that ran logging operations and the pulp-and-paper mills. The end of central state planning following the collapse of the Soviet Union created a regulatory vacuum in Russia's forest management. The Federal Forest Service still exists, but there is no consolidated federal structure responsible for the forest industry—only one economic ministry with no regional branches.

Because most timber companies are now privatized or independent and so many foreign interests are pouring into the country with open wallets, federal ministers have suddenly become outsiders in their own government—unable to reverse their eroding influence on major policy or funding decisions. The Federal Forest Service falls into this category: it has good financing but no influence on issues, so its lobby in the Russian parliament and the Duma is not strong. Sadly, when it comes to the Russian forest, the term "toothless bureaucrat" has a ring of authenticity.

One result of the regulatory vacuum is that the forest industry has suffered, like other aspects of the Russian economy, from widespread corruption. According to Dmitri Aksenov, former director of the Moscow-based Biodiversity Conservation Center, the main source of corruption is not the forestry companies but the Federal Forest Service. "There are a number of companies trying to work properly," he says. Greenpeace Russia's report on the Karelian Isthmus Commission, signed by the governor of Leningrad region, revealed several violations by the Federal Forest Service including black market trade and widespread bribery. In a country where wages are rock bottom, paychecks often take months to arrive, and opportunities for advancement are almost nonexistent, such stories have become familiar in many walks of life, not just forestry.

As well as corruption, the desperate state of the Russian economy has contributed to a lapse in ethical standards from which scientists are by no means immune. According to Andrei Laletin, the promise of big dollars from giant, private sector corporations has proved too tempting for some Ph.D. researchers—some of whom earn less than U.S.$100 a month. For the right price, says

Laletin, they're willing to produce fraudulent research results to lend credibility to a major industrial development that may have harmful effects on the environment. As an example, Laletin recalls a pulp mill not far from the Siberian town of Baikalsk (population 18,000), which is said to have contaminated the nearby Lake Baikal, the deepest lake in the world. To combat the growing pressure to close it down, the mill recently hired what Laletin calls a "handy scientist" to write an article saying that the water of Baikalsk was *too pure*—that pollution produced by the mill was like "vitamins" for the ecosystem.

RUSSIAN ROULETTE

Like their tropical counterparts in the Amazon, the boreal forests of Russia are huge reservoirs for carbon. But those reservoirs release carbon to the atmosphere when the forests are logged—a concern especially in Siberia, where 65 percent of boreal forests are located in the permafrost zone. When forests are logged, frozen soils are exposed to sunlight, causing the top layer of permafrost to melt. Soil erosion also becomes a problem, especially in mountainous regions where the tree cover is removed. Once these changes occur, the forest area converts to swampland, making reforestation impossible. Finally, when permafrost melting is accelerated, harmful concentrations of methane gas, mostly from the underlying peatlands, are released into the atmosphere.

Unfortunately, the country with the greatest stake in the study of boreal climate change is the furthest behind in research in the field. Following the collapse of the Soviet Union in 1991, the few scientists who had managed to set up a climate change research apparatus had their funding withdrawn and their projects dismantled. Since that time, cash-strapped climate scientists have often had to forge alliances with Western institutions. "It's hard to say whether they're connecting with Western scientists on climate change," says the University of British Columbia's Stewart Cohen. "The Russians," he says, "differ from the IPCC on climate change—they see it as a good thing. They're much more interested in long-term influences or orbital changes or solar output changes, because that's part of their scientific history. None of them do Western-style climate modeling—they don't have any ownership in that pool. Their ownership is looking at cosmic rays and solar cycles."

As with so many other aspects of the Russian taiga, climate change research is also affected by politics. Not long ago, a Japanese research team set up a joint study with Russian scientists in northern Siberia. Protocols were negotiated and funding was in place—but the project collapsed after little more than a year. The reason? Apparently, the ghosts of Soviet bureaucracy and KGB paranoia intruded on the proceedings. "Here's a Japanese group —very good scientists, very patient—and they sat down with their Russian colleagues," recalls the University of Alaska's Glenn Juday. "Well, they started the project in Russia and ran into enormous numbers of logistical and practical difficulties: permissions denied to travel, zealous Russian government officials being very suspicious about foreigners running around in their country, instrumentation that they think may have [had] some nefarious purpose. A friend of mine was actually detained because he had a high-precision GPS unit and that was considered a military threat." (A GPS uses satellite signals to determine the position on the earth's surface.)

When the scientists returned the second year, says Juday, the harassment got worse, so the project was canceled. It's a brick wall that scientists throughout the world encounter when they deal with Russian authorities. Western scientists helping a Russian project take it for granted that they (or their institution) will cover the costs—but might not return home with the equipment they brought. "You get the permission to *import* it," Juday laughs, summing up the bureaucratic mentality, "you just don't get the permission to *export* it."

Despite these facts, Russian legislators are allowing their

country's boreal forest to become a natural resource playpen for the world—a clearinghouse of timber, petroleum, and minerals for international investors. It's a colonial mentality that predates the arrival of the free-market system; as far back as 1990, the Soviet government was inviting foreign investment and joint ventures with European, Japanese, Korean, and North American timber companies. As one observer prophetically noted at the time:

> The boreal forests of the Soviet Union appear to be where the Amazon was 15 years ago. If we have learned anything from our experience in tropical rain forests, it is that large pristine areas can be jeopardized very quickly when national authorities decide their resources should be exploited.

But this analysis failed to anticipate the economic fallout of Russia's eventual transition to a free-market system. Faced with pervasive unemployment and poverty, food shortages, a worthless ruble, and a massive foreign debt, post-Soviet legislators are faced with the daily dilemma of how to create wealth and feed the Russian people without destroying the natural environment that represents so much potential richness. Under pressure by the World Bank and the International Monetary Fund, politicians have found that the temptation to sell off the country's resources is too great to resist. "Western collaboration and investment of course are needed," a former economic adviser to the Russian government told *Time* magazine. "But the Russians have been preoccupied with the fight for the spoils. No one is thinking of long-term strategy."

Until that mentality changes, the amount of forest preserved as parkland is unlikely to keep up with the rate of deforestation. Russia's great boreal forests, like the former Soviet system, will then exist only in its literature.

CHAPTER 7

Scandinavia:
The North's Plantation

What was needed was a methodical forestry that would, over time ... bring it into some kind of proper hierarchy ... [Tree] specimens of a like variety and maturity would present themselves in tidy battalions ready for their marching orders.

—Simon Schama, describing the scientific management approach to European forestry in the 19th century, from *Landscape and Memory*

In 1895, the Norwegian explorer Fridtjof Nansen boarded the ship *Fram* with a large crew, setting sail for a three-year journey into the Arctic. Near the beginning of the trip, Nansen and his men left the ship to wander the tundra of northern Siberia on dog-pulled sleds. Nansen marveled at the boreal life-forms he discovered sprouting through the snow—the "brownish green carpet of moss and grass that spread over the plain, bestrewn with flowers of rare beauty." Later he came upon an aboriginal "nomad" surrounded by a herd of reindeer. Recording the scene in his diary, he expressed the sweeping romanticism that has gripped so many travelers to the North:

Over these mighty tundra-plains of Asia, stretching infinitely onwards from one sky-line to the other, the nomad wanders with his reindeer herds, a glorious, free life! Where he wills he pitches his tent, his reindeer around him; and at his will again he goes on his way. I almost envied him. He has no goal to struggle towards, no anxieties to endure—he has merely to live!

Nansen published this passage in 1898 in a best-selling account of his expedition, *Farthest North,* a book that propelled its middle-aged author into fame and fortune. Nansen was one of a handful of writers who pioneered a literary tradition in Norway: a great outdoors genre emphasizing the "endless wilderness" of the Scandinavian North, its tundra, and its boreal forests. This genre inspired many who followed Nansen to describe their natural environment with expansive prose and earnest romanticism. It spawned a cultural mythology that remains potent in Norwegian society to this day.

Given the current state of that country's boreal forest (only 0.5 percent of Norway remains virgin forest), such mythology can have its drawbacks. If you're an ecologist trying to convince fellow citizens that the Norwegian boreal forest is not the sylvan utopia the tourism ministry makes it out to be, you face a big obstacle: an entire body of literature and painting dedicated to perpetuating the Norwegian stereotype of a great outdoors that hasn't changed in more than a hundred years.

"Our work is hard enough already," sighs Knut-Erik Helle, a member of the Norwegian Society for Nature Conservation. One of a dozen Norwegian activists arrested in the mid-1990s for halting a logging project, Helle is a front-line player in Norway's seemingly endless political tug-of-war: the struggle to capture the hearts and minds of the public in the debate about old-growth forests.

When I met Helle at the 4th Taiga Rescue Network conference, he told me how cultural mythology contributes to public apathy about Norwegian taiga forests. "The public is living this illusion that there's this endless Norwegian forest," he said. "But there's not much left of it. They're living in the past."

Norwegians do take pride in their mountainous landscape and beautiful coastline, Helle explained, but the state of the forests is often taken for granted. As long as the mountain forest ecosystems are saved, the thinking goes, that should be enough "biodiversity" to go around. It's that kind of thinking, says Helle, that would have writers like Nansen shaking their heads in dismay: "They would say, 'What is all this industry and clear-cutting?'"

They might ask the same about Sweden and Finland.

THE SCANDINAVIAN MODEL

The exploitation of the boreal forests of Scandinavia is at the opposite extreme from that of Siberia. Although the Russian forests are mostly still intact—current industrial activity having only begun the first stage of exploitation—virtually all the forest land of Sweden, Finland, and Norway has been converted into heavily managed second-growth woodlands. In Scandinavian countries, the remains of old-growth can best be described as "small and isolated islands within a sea of plantation-like forests." Russia and Canada may be the largest suppliers of boreal wood, but Scandinavia is not far behind: more than 30 percent of the United Kingdom's paper and more than 20 percent of its wood comes from the forests of Finland and Sweden. And although less than 5 percent of the land in each of the three Scandinavian countries is productive forest land (see Table 7.1), none of those countries has guaranteed the protection of old-growth forests.

Much of this problem can be attributed to a land use planning system known as the Scandinavian Model, an intensive method

Table 7.1 Area of Protected Productive Forest Land in Scandinavian Countries

	Area (in hectares)	Percentage of productive forest land
Finland	520,000	2.6
Sweden	832,000	3.6
Norway	62,000	1.06

(Source: Taiga Rescue Network)

of plantation forestry often credited with the disappearance of old-growth forests in Finland, Sweden, and Norway. The Scandinavian Model, perfected during the 1960s, is a system of logging in which one forest is cut and then replaced by seedlings; the process is then repeated in a neighboring forest. The model is based on the assumptions of sustained yield—the notion that reforestation alone is enough to preserve the biodiversity of a clear-cut forest.

But it hasn't turned out that way. Over the past thirty years, the logging industry has flourished while the Scandinavian boreal forest has been drained of its richness. Under the Scandinavian Model, deciduous tree types face extinction, and very few old or dead trees, wet forests, or burned areas are to be found. Instead, the Scandinavian taiga is composed of even-aged, single-species stands of coniferous trees that are harvested early in their life-span. Deciduous seedlings are often removed, and wet forest lands become a grid full of drainage ditches.

Old-growth forests can never be replaced by plantation forests because the latter cannot duplicate an ecosystem that contains trees of different ages or those that are dead and decaying. Old-growth boreal forests are biologically richer than plantation forests because they take centuries to develop and have a different assemblage of species. When an old-growth forest is wiped out by clear-cutting, the animal, plant, and fungi species are wiped out with it. Biodiversity disappears. Old-growth forests are also subject to wildfires, storms, insects, and fungi that alter the forest structure by killing and felling trees, which then enrich the soil, allowing new trees to spring up in the gaps. This cycle does not occur in the plantation forests.

Northern Scandinavia hasn't seen a large cover of virgin forest since the end of the 18th century, when human activity was limited to a local scale. The boreal forest began to disappear in the 19th century as a result of the widespread practice of timber mining, a logging method whereby a lumber company removed entire stands of forest before moving on to another pristine location. The first wave of timber mining moved from south to north. By the beginning of the 20th century, most of Finland's and Sweden's boreal trees were headed for sawmills; before long, the forest industry was confronted with a timber shortage.

The looming crisis prompted the next stage of Scandinavian forestry, the tree plantation phase. Tree seedlings were planted in the clear-cut areas to secure future timber supplies. Meanwhile, the logging continued at a frenzied pace. Forest legislation before 1994 in Sweden and before 1997 in Finland even stated that it was against the law *not* to harvest mature stands, according to Karin Lindahl of the Taiga Rescue Network.

Somewhat miraculously, reforestation managed to keep up with the increase in annual harvests of old-growth forests during the first half of the century. Thanks to the reforestation of agricultural land in the south, Scandinavia's stock of trees is increasing. But this endless cycle of clear-cutting and replanting cannot last forever. Today, old-growth areas are rapidly decreasing in size and number, and replacing them with plantations has led to a biodiversity crisis in Scandinavia. The Swedish Red Data List— an index that records endangered species—contains about seventeen hundred forest-dwelling species. "If the Scandinavian Model is sustainable in terms of continued timber supply," concludes the Taiga Rescue Network's Bjorn Lindahl, "it certainly isn't in terms of maintained space for the forests' organisms."

Finland: Trying to Have It Both Ways

In Finland, where 62 percent of the forest landscape is owned by individuals, the need to preserve forests is balanced with government efforts to stimulate business growth and serve the needs of small landowners. Thus, the forest legislation of 1997 was designed to achieve a compromise: preserving biodiversity in Finland's forests while ensuring the continuity of timber production.

But while protected areas were increased from 2.5 to 3.5 percent,

Finnish NGOs estimated that between 100,000 and 200,000 hectares (between 250,000 and 500,000 acres) of old-growth forest remained unprotected. Within those forests are now more than 700 plant and animal species, including the flying squirrel and golden eagle. Because of human activity, about 7 percent of the known species in Finland are in danger of disappearing. In almost half of these cases, forestry is the main cause. There are more than 135 threatened species inhabiting old-growth forests, almost half of them incapable of surviving elsewhere.

> *Because of human activity, about 7 percent of the known species in Finland are in danger of disappearing.*

Most of Finland's state lands, water, and forests are managed by the federal Forest and Park Service, formerly the National Board of Forestry. The Forest and Park Service is responsible for about 90 percent of the country's old-growth forest logging enterprises. In October 1997, the service—responding to criticism from conservationists—asked environmental groups to map the old-growth forests that remained unprotected. When the groups returned the completed maps three months later—demanding a two-year logging moratorium and the immediate protection of some 370 sites —the Forest and Park Service refused to respond. The logging continued, despite the objection of several major Dutch customers of the paper industry, who had twice appealed to the Forest and Park Service not to support logging in old-growth forests.

In recent years, the Forest and Park Service has promoted a controversial system known as ecological landscape planning. This method, adopted in Finland during the mid-1990s, when an old-growth protection program was being prepared on state land in the north, is supposed to improve forest management while protecting old-growth forests.

The government, hoping to appease the forest industry, pledged that not all old-growth forests in Finland would be protected. Ecological landscape planning bought politicians more time to determine the fate of the forest while offering a mixed-use alternative for state land that appears, on the surface, to protect more old-growth. Instead of employing the usual forestry standard of preserving a single old-growth patch of only a few hundred hectares, ecological landscape planning includes an assessment of the larger forest area to determine how various patches of old-growth within that area might be connected.

The government claims that ecological landscape planning will allow industry to survive while maintaining the features of old-growth forests. But a growing body of evidence suggests that this method only increases fragmentation while reducing the total area of a forest. According to University of Helsinki professor Ilkka Hanski, an "extinction wave" that has already depleted old-growth forests in the south is threatening to take over the northern boreal forest because several forests with ecological landscape planning appear to favor commercial forest management at the expense of old-growth trees and endangered species.

With ecological landscape planning, all unprotected old-growth forests within a designated area are supposed to remain standing, but without the legal status of a protected forest. But it hasn't turned out that way. According to the Finnish Nature League, the only old-growth forests left standing under this system are those with an active presence of NGO activists. "Basically what Ilkka Hanski's arguing [in his article] is that you can only save the species in old-growth forests by leaving the old-growth forest unlogged," says Kaisa Raitio of the Finnish Nature League. "And if you're carrying out an ecological plan *within* an old-growth spot—instead of having it as one element in a bigger plan—then of course you're splitting it up and you're just fragmenting, and it doesn't work. So his point is that if it's used to log any single old-growth forest, then it's working against its purpose."

Perhaps the Finnish government and forest industry—like their North American counterparts with their various "Share the Forest" schemes—will be doomed by a plan that tries to please everyone.

SWEDEN: MISTAKES MADE, LESSONS LEARNED

The next time you buy a piece of furniture from Ikea—or any other store selling wood products from Sweden—you may notice a label on the side that says FSC. That's the official seal of the Forest Stewardship Council, an independent international organization that certifies forest management according to strict ecological guidelines. On the surface, the FSC seal tells you that your product was not made from old-growth forests. It's also a guarantee that local aboriginal populations were consulted about logging operations, that workers' rights were respected, and that the logging company involved in preparing your product satisfied all FSC guidelines. Before deciding whether a forest product should be certified, FSC assessors evaluate how the forest where it came from is managed. Typically, they visit:

- A site where logging is happening or has occurred recently
- A site one or two years after logging (to check for regeneration)
- A site five to seven years after logging (to see how or whether the new stand has established itself)
- Riparian areas
- Places set aside as reserves
- Very hilly areas

As the first country in the world to enact such a process, Sweden has every right to be proud of the FSC standard. (Ironically, it is only one of two boreal countries with certified forests. In the temperate zone, nine countries have certified forests; in the tropics, fourteen countries have certified forests.) But the Forest

Stewardship Council was not just a progressive idea that grew out of nowhere. Largely a response to poor forestry practice in Sweden, it is only a beginning in the long-term effort to reverse two centuries of destruction in the Swedish taiga.

Like its Finnish and Norwegian cousins, Swedish forestry in the early 19th century shifted from small-scale local use (firewood, smelting houses, grazing, agriculture) to large-scale exploitation for commercial logging. The increasing international demand for sawn timber meant that high-quality, large-diameter pine began to disappear very quickly—most of it to supply the rapidly expanding sawmill industry. At the turn of the 20th century, a "second wave" of exploitation was aimed at spruce and smaller trees for the pulp-and-paper industry. This second wave used far more clear-cutting than the first.

"There were huge clear-cuts, which perhaps you see more of in North America," says Jan Henriksson, a member of the Swedish Society for Nature Conservation. During the 1960s and 1970s, the Swedish forest industry launched a full-scale attack on deciduous trees because the forestry market was focused on softwoods such as spruce and pine. To make room for softwood plantations, companies conducted widespread chemical spraying and a form of selective logging that rid the forest of trees considered too sick or decayed for commercial use. But this practice only served to eliminate most of Sweden's deciduous trees. As Karin Lindahl of the Taiga Rescue Network explains:

> Virtually every hectare of Swedish forest land has in some way been affected by human activities ... Today, Sweden is full of trees—but there is very little forest.

Economically, the Scandinavian Model has been a success in Sweden. Silvicultural methods such as chemical treatment of soil, drainage ditches, fertilization, and selective logging have been used intensively to maximize yield. Combined with an aggressive plantation campaign, these methods have given Swedish forestry an international reputation as a model of sustainability. What its supporters have often failed to mention, however, are the costs of killing all those deciduous trees:

- Hundreds of forest-dwelling fungi and beetles, woodpeckers, and tree-nesting birds face extinction.
- Sweden's eight thousand species of invertebrates may be reduced by three-quarters because of intensive silviculture.
- Swedish pulp-and-paper mills are forced to import large quantities of birch pulp wood from the Baltic states and Russia.

Consumer pressure—fueled, in large part, by NGO activist campaigns—has begun to make a difference. Public criticism of the forest industry began in the early 1970s when citizen groups occupied logging sites to stop aerial spraying with pesticides. By the 1980s, biodiversity was the top issue, as more scientific studies confirmed the extent of biological degradation in the boreal forest. In the early 1990s, international consumers of Swedish forest products—mainly from Germany and the United Kingdom—began to exert their influence through boycotts. These events led to the campaign for forest management certification (the FSC standard), which has only recently come into effect.

By summer 1998, the largest area of forest in the world certified under FSC criteria was in Sweden. It was owned by Assi Doman, one of two major forest companies fully FSC certified in Sweden. More than 5 million hectares (12.4 million acres) of company land —almost 25 percent of productive forest land in Sweden—was FSC certified, with Assi Doman managing 3.3 million hectares (8 million acres). As the World Wildlife Fund announced a new certification target of 25 million hectares (62 million acres) by the year 2001, there was much optimism surrounding FSC-endorsed certification in the boreal forest. From the World Bank's perspective, these figures meant that Scandinavian forests were well on their way to recovery and that global logging agreements needn't be threatened by the perceived lack of old-growth trees.

The system is by no means perfect. Some argue that the FSC process is being manipulated by uncertified landowners. In one case, in the old-growth Arvliden Forest in northern Sweden, one state landowner who wanted to log part of the forest hired a consultant to assess the logging area. According to Greenpeace activist Mats Abrahamsson, the consultant's opinion was presented as an FSC certification. "It is not right to use FSC as a tool to certify clearcutting," Abrahamsson wrote, in the *Taiga News*.

PROTECTED AREAS: AN ELUSIVE GOAL

Despite its international reputation for progressive politics, Sweden has one of the worst forest protection records in the boreal forest. Although 57 percent of the total land area is covered in productive forest, only 3.5 percent of that area is protected in nature reserves or national parks. Below the mountain area, in the lowlands favored by the forest companies, that figure drops to about 0.8 percent of total forested land.

These figures begin to make sense when one considers the importance of the forest products industry to the Swedish economy. Sweden is a leading exporter of pulp, paper, and wood. In 1996, two of the world's ten largest paper producers were Swedish (Stora, ranked fifth, and SCA, ranked seventh), and the export value for Swedish forest products (85 billion Crowns) equaled expenditures for all imports of oil, food, clothes, and radio and television equipment. Of Sweden's 8 million inhabitants, 200,000 people are directly or indirectly employed in the forest sector, which contributed 10 billion Crowns in federal taxes. In addition, every third export ship carries forest industry cargo, 35 percent of railway goods are forest and wood products, and about half the country's 450,000 kilometers (280,000 miles) of roadways are used for logging.

Another reason for Sweden's poor forest protection record may be land ownership. Only one-fifth of the Swedish forest is state owned (including the holdings of Assi Doman, a private enterprise company with the state as main shareholder). Most state forests are in the northern mountainous region, which accounts for 85 percent of the country's protected forest land. Of the remaining forests, nearly half are privately owned by individual landowners; one-quarter by large forest companies (mostly in the north, where the remaining old-growth is located), and the remaining 8 percent by other public bodies such as churches and local municipalities.

"Nowadays there are small landowners—or perhaps medium-sized landowners—who have old-growth left and are more dependent on this particular land than the big companies [which] can log other areas," Jan Henriksson of the Swedish Society for Nature Conservation told me in Estonia. "But the landowners have to get paid in some way for forest protection. The government hasn't put enough money into that." Therein lies the problem.

In 1997, a federally funded scientific report recommended that 5 percent of Sweden's forest land below the mountain area be saved. Although the news was encouraging, it came with a warning: Sweden's last remaining old-growth forests would only be saved if that 5 percent figure were reached within the next ten years. Before this report, the federal budget allowed only $200 million Swedish Crowns (U.S.$25 million) annually to purchase forests from private landowners. By the end of summer 1998, the government promised to double that figure. "It's an expensive process," says NGO activist Jonas Rudberg. "That is the budget money that they have to protect forests all over Sweden, and that gives us a new few thousand hectares a year. But it will take many, many years to protect all the 5 percent that is definitely needed in the ten-year period." As the logging continues, the forest is in a race against the clock.

Swedish activists such as Rudberg and Henricksson are encouraged by the government's decision to shell out big money for forest protection (some estimates peg the new annual limit at U.S.$500 million), but the problem doesn't end there. "The most important thing now," adds Rudberg, "is to push for a moratorium—that everyone promise not to log and really do that."

To encourage a moratorium, the Taiga Rescue Network has sent an urgent message to the Swedish government, forest companies, small landowners, and timber consumers: Do not log or buy timber from Swedish old-growth forests.

THINKING SMALL: LANDOWNER COOPERATIVES AND COMMUNITY FORESTS

The best hope for a rejuvenated boreal forest in Scandinavia may be found in the practice of community forestry and in small landowner cooperatives. As home-grown alternatives to the Scandinavian Model of large-scale logging and reforestation, these ideas have already begun to flourish in Sweden, where until the 1930s forestry was dominated by the state.

During the Depression, Swedish farmers throughout the country began to organize agricultural cooperative societies, including forest owners associations. At first, the main purpose of these cooperatives was to obtain better prices for timber by coordinating supply and price negotiations. But by the 1950s, as farming was on the decline and the demand for Swedish wood products was on the rise, forest owners associations began to expand their harvesting and service organizations.

Today, some eight forest owners associations operate in two hundred forestry districts throughout Sweden. These associations have 88,000 members dividing some 5.6 million hectares (13.8 million acres) of total forest area. The average area is more than 60 hectares (150 acres). Although the primary aim of these associations is to promote the economic interests of its members, sustainable forest management is by no means a conflicting interest.

In fact, the associations incorporate "good forestry management" in their official principles. One example is the reduction of waste through the use of wood fuel in addition to sawn timber and pulp wood. "Stagnating or reduced demand and increasing quality requirements for [sawn timber] both creates a need and an opportunity for energy production based on silvicultural products," says Ulf Osterblom, of the National Federation of Forest Owners in Stockholm. "At present, the use of forest fuel, including bark and waste products from saw mills, amounts to almost 20 million cubic meters."

Private landowner cooperatives provide a variety of services for the average farm owner. They offer technical assistance and planning, education, government lobbying, product marketing, and even fee-for-service land work. "It's basically a one-stop shop—they're extremely successful, extremely powerful," says Paul Mitchell-Banks, a forestry consultant based in Vancouver, British Columbia. Just how powerful? Mitchell-Banks recalls a conversation he had with a cooperative executive at a 1994 conference in Poland. "He said the government, under pressure from industry, had been putting an awful lot of pressure on the cooperatives to back off, because they were [exercising] too much power."

In Sweden, individual forest owners in cooperation have a direct impact on the development their country's forestry and its forest industry. Collective ownership of forests in Sweden takes two forms. Common forests are owned by groups of landowners, while community forests are owned by the municipal government or the Lutheran church—still an influential institution in many parts of rural Sweden. Both types of forest ownership reflect the communalism that has dominated Swedish life for centuries. And the people take pride in their forest management: in some community offices, record keeping is so meticulous that logging records date back several decades.

Unlike the common forests, community forests run by municipalities, counties, or churches do not offer special, exclusive, or hereditary rights to harvest wood or hunt game. Instead, they serve as a source of timber products, employment, and recreation for the community. The city of Norberg, with its 30,000 hectares (75,000 acres) of forest land, provides Christmas tree harvesting, large and small-scale production of firewood, and traditional fencing modified for modern housing. As important is the recreational element of community forests. Throughout Sweden, community forests provide ideal conditions for cross-country skiing in the winter, mushroom and berry-gathering in the summer, and walking and hiking in spring and fall. Immediate access to the forest is of crucial importance for Sweden's increasingly urban population. People want to enjoy the outdoors without having to drive great distances. That's why, in Sweden, the community forest often begins right outside the front door and the so-called green corridor of forest often extends into the urban center. This type of urban forest can be found in Stockholm, Sundsvall, and Umea in Sweden; Joensuu and Helsinki in Finland; and Drammen and Oslo in Norway.

Throughout Sweden, community forests provide ideal conditions for cross-country skiing in the winter, mushroom and berry-gathering in the summer, and walking and hiking in spring and fall.

Approached in this way, community forests and urban expansion need not be mutually exclusive. Community forests preserve valuable urban green space while promoting economic goals such as increased densification, reduced municipal servicing costs, and limited urban fringe growth. It's an approach to forestry that has attracted much attention internationally. As Mitchell-Banks has noted: "Many community forests have a policy that for every hectare released from the community forest to urban development, a replacement hectare has to be purchased, resulting in no net loss to the community forest area."

The community forest concept is not foolproof. When community politicians are keen to maximize potential revenues from timber harvests, they don't always consider the potential impact on forest, as at least one case in Norway has demonstrated. But for the most part, the Swedish people are happy with the community forest model. Municipalities use either their own staff or a management company to manage the forest according to the policies established by the municipal council. Any net profit from the community forest ends up with the community.

The community forest plan is set for a ten-year period. Annual reviews are held and public input is welcome at every stage. But despite this open door policy—the community has access to all the relevant documentation and plans for the forest—little public input is ever provided. As Mitchell-Banks explains, the Swedish public is "generally pleased" with present community forest management. "Small-scale forestry," he told me in an interview, "has demonstrated its capacity to deal with the transition from old-growth to second-growth because of the diversity of management strategies and timing—the experimentation that's gone on, and the importance of forestry as part of the community culture, which isn't the case here in Canada. I've been arguing this for years: we think we're a forest nation, but we're not. We're still very much in a pioneering mentality—that the forests are a barrier we have to cut down."

NORWEGIAN FORESTS:
A PRIVATE OWNER'S DREAM

Norway is one of the richest countries in the world. It has a booming export in industrial goods, the fourth largest merchant fleet in the world, and no debt. It has an almost zero inflation rate, and 45 percent of its GDP comes from foreign trade, yet it has the worst forest protection record of any boreal country.

Forests and other woodlands account for about 37 percent of the Norwegian mainland. Of this area, about 23 percent is considered productive forest; 5 percent is classified as old-growth. Private ownership is much more prevalent than in Sweden or Finland; roughly 80 percent of Norway's forests are privately owned. Ten percent are state lands, another 5 percent belong to companies, and the remainder belong to municipalities.

Norway contains the world's northernmost pine forests and several forests unique to Europe. This boreal region is the main European source of about sixty species of lichens and mosses. Biologists have found remnants of old-growth forests in the southeast that are several centuries old, comparable to those found in Poland and Belarus.

Only 1 percent of Norwegian forest land is protected. Scientists believe that a minimum of 5 percent of productive forest area should be protected, but government has no plans to reach this goal. Meanwhile, the small stands of remaining old-growth are nearly gone. Between 1990 and 1995, massive clear-cut logging and road construction destroyed or fragmented at least 90 percent of the old-growth stands mapped during the 1940s.

Only 1 percent of Norwegian forest land is protected.

Recently, the government announced a plan to clear a 750-square-kilometer (290-square-mile) tract of forest in the south, along the Swedish border, to make way for a new military target field. The area, still under construction, will be used for all military weaponry over the next decade. New high-tech missiles will be projected over civilian areas at a 50-kilometer (30-mile) range. The area is also the most important wintering area for bears and moose in southern Norway. All the country's large beasts of prey —brown bear, lynx, wolverine, and wolf—can be found here. The area is filled with vast forests of pine and spruce. Most sensitive are the deep bogs, which are not expected to tolerate heavy vehicle traffic. Workers who conducted an environmental impact assessment concluded that the area was valuable and should be preserved. Understandably, the government's plan has prompted an international campaign by Norwegian conservation groups.

One of the biggest obstacles to forest protection is Norway's archaic forestry legislation. Dating back to 1965, its main purpose is forest production, not protection. Environmental protection provisions amount to little more than finger wagging: industry should take "reasonable care" when logging. Under this carte blanche arrangement, landowners aren't required to apply to authorities before logging unless the forest is classified as a poor growing area. This arrangement makes it even more difficult for NGOs to monitor industrial activity in old-growth forests. "Foresters don't have to send in a message saying, 'Well, now I've started logging; now I'm finished logging,'" says Knut-Erik Helle of the Norwegian Society for Nature Conservation. "So we have a thousand-plus areas with old-growth forests, but we don't know the status if you can't go there and have a look."

Because there is almost no state-owned forest land in Norway, pushing for change means convincing approximately 130,000 small landowners that forest preservation is in their best interests. But many owners of large forest property have close ties with the forest industry, and government provides a lot of incentives to do business. In Norway's western pine forests and mixed pine/deciduous forests, for example, the agriculture department subsidizes road building, logging, and transfers of exotic tree species into monoculture forests. Many of these landowners realize that the trees on their property can bring huge profits if they are used to feed Norway's pulp-and-paper mills. Because the federal agriculture department has a strong influence on the government, landowners also know that they will have no trouble selling or leasing their forest land. The pulp-and-paper industry has become so powerful that Norwegian forest law is managed by the agricultural ministry.

Understandably, this cozy relationship is cause for much cynicism in Norwegian conservation circles. According to Helle, the main reason Norway lacks an effective environmental lobby group is that most environmentalists believe that governmental lobbying is futile—even counterproductive. Working within the system, in this case, would mean compromising the future of the forest. In contrast to Germany, a more industrialized country whose mass destruction in World War II and current environmental problems have led to a heightened awareness of the need to preserve forests and other ecosystems (thus producing a strong environmental lobby that has influenced policy and led to the first Green Party–led coalition government in the Western world), Norway is less urbanized and industry in general enjoys more support among the population.

Thus, groups such as the Norwegian Society for Nature Conservation prefer to focus their efforts on educating the public rather than on gaining access to government corridors more friendly to industry. "Norway has the most open social democratic political system in the world," says Helle. "I think it's important to be on the outside [as a conservationist]. To be a sort of watchdog that's truly free of commitments with government and industry."

Right now, Helle's group is trying to raise awareness about the activities of Norway's leading manufacturer of pulp and paper. Norske Skog accounts for 60 percent of the country's total annual harvest in its mills. Almost half of the company's production is exported to Western Europe for newsprint, mainly to Germany and the U.K. Norske Skog's customers include the British newspapers the *Guardian* and *Daily Express,* and the German publishing house Axel Springer Verlag. Axel Springer has declared its intention to deal only with "clear-cut free" paper product. Despite such public statements, however, its supplier has made no such commitment. Norske Skog got into trouble in 1997 when it was revealed that the company had purchased timber from Skotjern-fjell, a small old-growth area close to Oslo. The area had been declared a national treasure by environmental authorities and was under consideration for protection. Norske Skog had assured its customers that it would not buy timber from such places. When NGO activists learned in April 1997 that the company had gone into Skotjernfjell, a boycott became inevitable. Since then, the company has done an about-face, officially declaring that logging in areas such as Skotjernfjell is not consistent with sustainable forestry.

Fighting Norske Skog's logging operations in old-growth forests is about to become a much bigger challenge. In February 1999, the company established a newsprint joint venture known as the Pan Asia Paper Company (PAPCO), a merger of Norske Skog, Abitibi-Consolidated (Canada), and Hansol Paper (Korea). Norske Skog CEO Jan Reins boasted of the merger as a "major step in the global consolidation of the paper industry," noting that his company had already been running two PAPCO mills in Korea and Thailand for half a year and that more than half its newsprint capacity was outside Norway. PAPCO's total tonnage for sale would be approximately 1.8 million tonnes, or some 30 percent of the market share in the Asia Pacific region outside Japan. "In less than ten years, we have more than doubled our newsprint capacity and developed from being a medium-sized supplier with mills in Norway to one of the leading global players," said Reins. Missing from the corporate bulletin was any mention of company policy on old-growth forests.

In 1996, the government announced that it would increase protected coniferous forests in Norway by 12,000 hectares (30,000 acres)—pushing the total protected area up to 1.06 percent of productive forest land. This gesture seemed rather meaningless, coming from a government that had signed the convention on biodiversity. "Norwegian authorities are quick to criticize countries such as Brazil for their destruction of rainforests," concludes activist Rein Midteng. "[But] most of the [Norway's] remaining old growth forests will be gone within the next five years. Norway has the money, but lacks the will to stop this devastating process."

GOOD FORESTS MAKE BAD NEIGHBORS: SCANDINAVIAN INDUSTRY IN RUSSIA

The Scandinavian Model of forestry could just as well apply to old-growth logging or the purchase of old-growth products in the Russian taiga as it does to Scandinavian silviculture and plantation forestry. For all its claims about respecting biodiversity at home, the forest products industry of Finland, Sweden, and Norway has not hesitated to clear-cut old-growth forests in Russia. Companies such as ENSO, UPM, Norske Skog, Assi Doman, SCA, Stora, and Modo operate with impunity in cash-poor countries such as Russia, where labor is cheap, environmental laws are almost nonexistent, and old-growth forests are plentiful.

Some might even argue—as a 1992 editorial in the Swedish forestry magazine *Skogen* (*The Forest*) did—that the green movement inadvertently did industry a big favor by pressuring companies to abandon domestic operations. By expanding internationally, the forest industry could afford to promote its use of "green" products at home without having to depend on a long-since-depleted forest ecosystem. But sooner or later, the forest companies' operations in Russia would catch up to them.

The presence of companies such as ENSO, Norske Skog, and Assi Doman in the Russian taiga signifies a major shift in Scandinavian forest politics: three countries once renowned for their vast resources of timber have become major consumers of boreal forests. Finland is the biggest consumer of all.

Although Japan accounts for 42 percent of all Russian exports of raw logs, Finland now comes in a close second at 39 percent. Of all the timber that leaves the Russian northwest, Finland's take is more than 90 percent. And ENSO, the pulp-and-paper giant, takes nearly half that amount.

In 1997, ENSO declared a logging moratorium in the old-growth forests of Karelia, a nonautonomous Russian republic that lies along the Finnish border between Murmansk in the north and St. Petersburg in the south. Karelia is part of a large forest ecosystem that forms the Green Belt of Fennoscandia: a 1200-kilometer (750-mile) stretch of unfragmented and nearly untouched natural forests that lie along the border dividing Russia from Finland and Norway. Encompassing an area where only small patches of old-growth forests remain, the Green Belt stretches from the Gulf of Finland in the south to the Barents Sea in the north. Distinct enough to be recognizable in satellite images, it crosses several ecological regions from taiga to tundra.

Before the Soviet era, northwestern Russia was a closed primeval forest, with only a small population of Karelians surviving by farming. The present border area was excluded from logging because its forests were too remote and transport across rivers was difficult. During the Soviet era, the inhabitants of the border area to the west were moved out and villages were converted to military stations. The entire border zone was closed, and virtually no forest operations were allowed. By the end of the Cold War, land use had been almost nonexistent for half a century.

But all that changed with the opening of the Soviet republics. With the introduction of free enterprise, the Green Belt's unique location along the border turned its forests into a logical destination for international logging and mining interests. Because the former Soviet state forestry companies were no longer profitable, the domestic market was collapsing throughout the country. By the early 1990s, the Finnish export market was looking very attractive to Russian forest officials. "Instead of preserving and supporting the local wood processing industry," reports the Taiga Rescue Network's Eva Kleinn, "Russia trie[d] to make quick profits in foreign currency by exporting the unprocessed raw material in order to fill up the empty state accounts. The pressure on border forests such as the Green Belt is especially high because of the short distance to Finland."

When large-scale logging began in the Green Belt, most of the timber came from old-growth forests—in some cases from existing conservation areas. For this reason, scientists and eco-activists have applied for the designation of UNESCO World Heritage Site for the Green Belt. If the campaign works, vast areas of Russian old-growth taiga may be spared from logging.

One of the many people fighting to preserve the Green Belt was Otso Ovaskainen, now a mathematics professor and member of the Finnish Nature League. Ovaskainen was among the dozens of Finnish activists who, in the early 1990s, set up camp along the Russian border to protest the logging of Karelian old-growth forests. I met Ovaskainen, one of the Taiga Rescue Network's main contacts in Finland, at the conference in Estonia in October 1998.

Sitting in a pub late one afternoon following a long day of conference seminars, Ovaskainen told me how the Finnish people feel a special obligation to protect Russian old-growth forests. This sense of duty owed something, he said, to the historical relationship between the two countries. Before World War II, the Finnish border extended beyond Karelia into what became the Soviet Union and is now still part of Russia. According to Ovaskainen, there are a lot of Finnish villages in Karelia, and the Karelian language is very similar to Finnish. So the people, he says, "are carrying on with the same culture that was there before the war—that's very important for us."

But Finland's approach to Karelia is freighted with paternalism. In the forests immediately surrounding the protected areas, said Ovaskainen, "Finnish industry is still saying 'We have to operate in Karelia, because it's so poor. We have to help them.' But it's really not the case, what they're doing." These days, Finnish companies arrive in the Russian forest in Finnish trucks driven by

Finns, carrying Finnish machinery and Finnish workers. The Russian roundwood they log is brought back to Finland, where it's processed to serve the Finnish economy.

"When you think of what's left to Karelia or to Russia," Ovaskainen concludes, "it's not much. Some money for the logging ticket, but that's all. So it's not helping Russia. And if you think how poor Russia is and how rich Finland is, it's really something that shouldn't happen. What should be done is that the local people employ themselves by the wood trade, making some money processing wood in Russia, then maybe exporting it, but that's really not the case today." The Finnish forest industry is moving even farther to the east, toward areas where no logging moratoriums exist and where there are no guarantees that the wood does not come from old-growth forests.

Karelia is one of the most important biodiversity centers in Europe. In Finland's southern Lapland, an old-growth forest of 10,000 hectares (25,000 acres) is considered large; but in Russian Karelia, there are forests of 100,000 to 200,000 hectares (250,000 to 500,000 acres)—all of them untouched woodlands. These same forests contain a large number of threatened animal species. "If you think about those species that you have in the taiga," Ovaskainen says, "all the threatened species are found in Karelia. On the Finnish side, you might also have those species there, but they are nearer to being extinct. In Russian Karelia, you still have areas where they live quite well."

The Paanajarvi region, with its healthy water routes, productive fishing, and rich game stocks, has been settled for more than seven thousand years.

Some Karelian villages originate from the Soviet era, but many are centuries old, their inhabitants direct descendants of the original Karelians. The Paanajarvi region, with its healthy water routes, productive fishing, and rich game stocks, has been settled for more than seven thousand years. In the Viena region of Karelia, some villages have remained intact for up to five hundred years. The people in these villages survived by cultivating, grazing, forestry, reindeer herding, hunting, fishing, berry picking, and small-scale logging. It was a thriving boreal culture that inspired Finnish artists, including the painter Akseli Gallen-Kallela, whose *Shepherd Boy from Paanajarvi* and *Great Black Woodpecker* are considered major works. During the 1920s and 1930s, Kalevala National Park had as many as five thousand inhabitants. Since then, as clear-cutting has torn away the forest and moved closer to the villages, the population has dwindled to less than seven hundred. Nearly everyone is opposed to the clear-cutting. In Karelia, it is said, people know the difference between a natural environment and a manipulated one.

In this economically depressed region, Russian timber companies are forced to engage in ethically questionable arrangements just to keep afloat. Nikolai Kalinin, director of a regional state company that sells wood for a small community in northwestern Karelia, told a local newspaper reporter how his company gets its tractors: "A Petrozavodsk company, Valentina, supplies Onega tractor factory with steel, Onega supplies us with tractors and we pay Valentina by giving them wood."

Kalinin was asked about the rows of expensive new cars lining the roads of Borovoi and even sitting in his office parking lot. Who did they belong to? "Most of them are strictly our enemies," he said. "Cutting tickets have been given for about 30 enterprises ... Most of these enterprises are not Karelian." In no time at all, he said, foreign interests had taken over Karelian roads and were now cutting down the forests the local people had spared for bad days in the future. "Another ten years of this kind of robbery," Kalinin concluded, "and we can say that Borovoi, Jyskyjarvi, and new Jyskyjarvi, will be left totally unemployed."

Victory in the Taiga:
A Moratorium for the Green Belt

Until the end of 1996, there were no logging moratoriums in northwestern Russia. The country itself was virtually invisible on the World Heritage Site map. Even though it covers one-eighth of the world's surface, Russia had no influence on the heritage preservation lottery because it lacked the human and financial capacity to prepare nomination papers and hadn't paid its UNESCO contributions in years. More recently, though, some progress has been made. In 1992, the country's Environmental Protection Act defined major types of specially protected natural areas. The highest protection category, known in Russian as *zapovednik,* was federal territory that could be used only as parkland. In March 1995, the government passed a law that regulates the organization, protection, and use of natural resources. Around the same time, regional parks were introduced, private property on protected territory was prohibited, and the government asked Greenpeace Russia to prepare nomination documents for eight potential World Heritage Sites. By early 1996, a group including NGOs and leading scientists from Russia and Finland agreed on a temporary list of thirty-five potential sites. The Green Belt was one of them.

During this time, Greenpeace Russia conducted massive public-awareness campaigns on the region. By 1996, ENSO (the Finnish forest giant most responsible for depleting Karelian old-growth forest) issued a challenge to the NGO community: the company would stop logging or buying timber from Karelian old-growth forests if the NGO community would define what it meant by "old-growth" and identify those forests in Karelia. The NGOs—somewhat stunned by their good fortune—jumped at the chance.

During summer 1997, two Russian NGOs—Greenpeace Russia and the Biodiversity Conservation Center (BCC)—published a map showing potentially valuable forest areas in Karelia. The map was based mostly on satellite images and forestry maps covering 1 million hectares (2.5 million acres) in Karelia. "That map was given to ENSO," Otso Ovaskainen explains, "and ENSO said, 'Okay. We accept this map, and we won't log here.'" After that decision, more than ten major forest companies in Finland joined the moratorium, which was later extended to include old-growth forests in Murmansk. Similar plans were drawn up for the Leningrad region.

Despite the victory, the largest old-growth forests in Karelia remain outside the moratorium area. In one 300,000-hectare (740,000-acre) forest, two-thirds of the area is open to logging; the remaining one-third is protected as national park space. One of ENSO's Russian customers has already begun logging in this forest, putting the Finnish pulp-and-paper giant in a difficult position: "ENSO is committed to the moratorium," says Ovaskainen. "It should stop buying from this Russian company." Another problem: the moratorium only applies to the Russian side of the border. The Finnish side of the Green Belt contains approximately 200,000 hectares (494,000 acres) of unprotected old-growth forest, but you won't hear ENSO talk of a moratorium at home.

Despite the victory, the largest old-growth forests in Karelia remain outside the moratorium area.

Two main problems must be overcome if Karelia is to avoid the fate of northern Finland. First, Finnish loggers can get prime Russian Karelian wood at a fraction of the world price by making handsome payoffs to corrupt Russian bureaucrats. Second, there's a lot of support for current logging practices among Karelian politicians, some of whom attribute Finland's wealth to good forestry. But this view is outdated, according to Finnish NGOs.

"They are thirty years behind—they don't understand the kind of problems we actually suffer at the moment because of so-called effective forestry," said Virpi Sahi, another member of the

Finnish Nature League. "This is the thing they do not inform the population about. They only [say] it's all about cutting forests and getting rich. But Finland and Karelia are totally different—the case of Finland cannot be repeated in Karelia."

As the campaign to preserve the Green Belt shows, protection of boreal forests is requiring more of a cooperative effort between the nations that produce those forests and the nations that consume them. As trade barriers fall, more and more citizens are finding that they have a stake in the future of communities and ecosystems beyond their own borders.

It's a dynamic the people of Alberta can appreciate only too well, thanks to the presence of Japanese timber and petroleum multinationals in the boreal forests north of Edmonton.

CHAPTER 8

Alberta:
Industry's Playground

It's the last big land grab. The boreal forest, auctioned off at the lowest prices anywhere; Premier Ralph Klein, receiver in bankruptcy, says: "Everything must go."

—Elizabeth May, *At the Cutting Edge:
The Crisis in Canada's Forests*

When British Columbian eco-activist Colleen McCrory coined the term "Brazil of the North" in 1993—launching a public-awareness campaign about clear-cut logging in her home province—she could also have been referring to British Columbia's neighbor to the east, Alberta. By the late 1990s, less than 9 percent of Alberta's woodlands could be described as wilderness. And the boreal forest in Alberta—which accounts for nearly one-tenth of the great Canadian taiga—was being cleared faster than the Brazilian rain forest.

According to an Environmental Protection Branch report to the Alberta government, the rates of attrition in the boreal forest resulting from climate change and industrial activity "almost match and exceed those reported for Amazonia from 1975 to 1988." The area of boreal forest logged annually increased by 125 percent between 1975 and 1993. As Edmonton forest ecologist Kevin Timoney said, "We have an exponential rising rate of cutting with no sign of leveling off. Unfortunately, most people know more about what's happening in the Amazon than in Alberta."

In 1975, Alberta was cutting 4 million cubic meters (5.2 million cubic yards) of wood a year. Twenty years later, the annual cut was more than 20 million cubic meters (26 million cubic yards). This orgy of cutting is matched by oil and mining exploration; more than 75 percent of Alberta's 4005 boreal townships now have oil wells, and more than 71 percent of them are fragmented by roads. Nearly three-quarters of the forest is leased for logging, drilling, and mining—or a combination of all three. Even provincial parkland isn't spared from industrial plundering; most of the boreal region's thirty-three parks contain at least one logging, mining, or oil operation. These are just a few of the reasons that the Sierra Club of the United States has referred to Alberta as the worst jurisdiction in North America for protecting the environment.

Following are some examples of the developments ripping apart the boreal forests of Alberta as the 1990s drew to a close:

- The Peace River region lost almost half of its original spruce and aspen over the previous forty years.
- Athabaska–Lac La Biche lost nearly 40 percent of its forest since 1940.
- Lesser Slave Lake Provincial Park contained a hundred active and inactive well sites.
- Seismic lines crisscrossed nearly 500,000 kilometers (over 300,000 miles) of forest.
- Pipelines cut across 73,102 kilometers (45,425 miles) of forest to serve 88,566 well sites, 160 gas-processing plants, and 26 oil and gas waste-treatment plants.
- As many as 200,000 trees were being sacrificed for every mining site that was cleared in the forest.
- Between 15 and 20 percent of loggable timber was being consumed by the construction of well sites and seismic lines.

Alberta's northern forests are like a fresh carcass in a desert full of vultures. Competing industrial interests are overlapping each other's projects to consume vast quantities of boreal resources, making it impossible to protect the forest. As one leading ecologist told the *Globe and Mail,* Alberta used "optimistic and simplistic math" when it doled out timber licenses in the 1990s. The government never considered how an increase in boreal forest fires, combined with the effects of mushrooming oil development projects, could deplete the forest beyond its ability to regenerate. "We have foreclosed on some future security for Albertans," said Brad Stelfox, a consultant to Daishowa-Marubeni. "And that's really sad."

Mortgaging the Future

Perhaps saddest of all is that most of the destruction of the boreal forest in Alberta has occurred in the past two decades and, with a bit of foresight, could have been prevented. During the mid-1980s, the provincial government adopted an aggressive strategy for industrial use of the forest to stimulate the economy. In one federal-provincial joint program, Alberta provided research and development funding to adapt Japanese technology to the pulping of aspen, which dominated the province's postfire second-growth forests. Aspen was once considered a weed species by a forest industry that preferred softwoods. But with a brand-new technology adding value to it—and a better stumpage rate to go along with it—aspen became the carrot that Alberta dangled before Japanese and U.S.-based pulp-and-paper giants. It was just a taste of the 87 percent of Alberta forests that the government was putting up for sale as Crown land.

The strategy worked. Between 1986 and 1994, more than Cdn. $3.7 billion in new investments were made in Alberta's forest industry when the government sold nearly one-fifth of the province to create seven new and two renegotiated Forest Management Agreements, each with a renewable twenty-year license. Part of the deal included Cdn.$1 billion in federal and provincial loans and subsidies. Before long, there were two new bleached-kraft pulp mills (two existing ones were expanded), two new chemical-thermal-mechanical pulp (CTMP) mills, one new mill for oriented strand board (a combination of wood products), and several new or expanded sawmills.

Bleached-kraft pulp mills and CTMP mills are frequently cited by environmentalists for their toxic hazards. Kraft pulp, used for a range of materials from cardboard boxes and brown paper bags to high-quality writing paper, is the strongest pulp. During the chlorine bleaching stage at the kraft mill, toxic chemical compounds, including dioxins and furans, are formed. These compounds are released in effluent, which ends up in the streams and rivers, killing fish and other aquatic life. CTMP mills, used to create diaper fluff, tissue, and newsprint (newsprint is made from a combination of kraft and CTM pulp), produce resins and fatty acids, that end up in water effluent when the pulp is washed. Both types of mills release sulfur dioxide and other vapors that cause a multitude of health problems in humans: respiratory ailments such as asthma, bronchitis, and emphysema, as well as cardiac problems. Thus, the concentration of so many mills in northern Alberta has raised concerns about the health of both the environment and the people living in it.

Most of the new developments were owned, in whole or in part, by three Japanese transnational timber companies: Mitsubishi, Honshu Paper, and Daishowa-Marubeni. By this time, Japan had become the top consumer of boreal wood products in Alberta.

PAPER TIGERS

On the face of it, Japan and Alberta seem the unlikeliest of trading partners. Japan is a small island country in Asia with centuries of tradition and an urbanized high-tech economy; Alberta is a large province in North America with only 130 years of recorded history and a resource-based economy. But each has something the other doesn't have: Alberta has oil and boreal forests aplenty, while Japan has money. In today's global trade market, that's a marriage made in heaven.

Japan is the largest importer of wood products in the world. This fact might seem surprising, because nearly 70 percent of the Japanese landscape is forested. About half of these forests are spruce; the other half consist of broad-leaved trees. The northern island of Hokkaido is almost completely covered in boreal forest. But today most of Japan's spruce trees are less than forty years old. They are to be found in plantation forests, part of a national reforestation campaign that followed the massive logging of the country's forests before and during World War II.

Alberta has oil and boreal forests aplenty, while Japan has money. In today's global trade market, that's a marriage made in heaven.

After losing its timber-rich colonies of Korea and the Sakhalin Islands in the war, Japan was forced to increase its use of domestic forests and waste paper to meet the country's growing demand for paper and packaging. By the mid-1960s, Japan's forests could no longer satisfy the increasing demand of the paper companies. So the companies began importing wood chips from temperate and tropical rain forest countries.

At the same time, the Japanese government and Japanese trading companies were beginning a series of large-scale development projects with the Soviet Union. These long-term compensation deals provided Japan with Russian raw materials and gave the Soviet Union Japanese machinery and low-interest loans from the Japanese government.

But the only "machinery" the Russians ever received was logging and harvesting equipment. Japan had its own value-added forest products industry to support; the last thing it wanted to do was hand over its latest processing technology to the Russians. So Japan's competitive trade policy slowed the growth of the Russian timber-processing industry, creating a dependence on raw-log exports that has further depleted the Russian taiga. After the logs arrived in Japan, they were immediately converted to value-added products and sold for up to ten times the cost of the timber. Not surprisingly, this situation hasn't helped trade relations between the two countries. By the mid-1990s, a series of disputes had led to the arbitration courts. Those disputes involving timber exports were usually prompted by Japanese complaints about poor quality and unsorted logs and were usually resolved by reducing the price paid by the Japanese. The Russians, for their part, complained that Japanese companies changed their names, dissolved, or otherwise disappeared after accepting huge payments.

In 1980, the domestic logging industry in Japan suffered a major blow when the United States pushed the Japanese government to reduce tariffs to balance the trade deficit. Since then, Japan's raw-log imports have shown no signs of slowing down. But Japanese industry representatives are loath to discuss the environmental implications of this trend. When asked by a conservation group what kind of Russian timber products it imported, the Sumitomo Corporation replied: "Information on imports, including lumber that we deal with, is an industrial secret. Therefore, our company does not officially announce information relating to tree species, past import records, and transaction policies concerning timber imports." Not to conservation groups, anyway.

Over the last fifteen years, tropical timber imports in Japan have gone down while temperate and boreal timber imports have gone up. Russian exports to Japan—which suffered a brief decline in the aftermath of the collapse of the Soviet Union— have since risen to all-time highs. Sawn wood imports from the United States and Canada have also gone up. In the last quarter century, substantial profits and a high rate of growth in the industry have allowed some of the leading Japanese pulp-and-paper companies to expand their domestic processing operations while building or purchasing mills overseas. That's where Alberta comes in.

During the late 1980s, Mitsubishi and Honshu formed one company, Alberta Pacific (Al-Pac), and immediately set about planning construction of a pulp mill on the Athabasca River. Touting Al-Pac as the largest single-line bleached-kraft pulp mill in the world, the company should have known it was courting controversy. The Athabasca River is a major tributary to the Mackenzie River Basin, which covers 570,000 square kilometers (220,000 square miles) of Canada's North. In 1990, an environmental assessment established that the Athabasca contained high levels of dioxins and furans and that the project should not proceed. In response, the Alberta government set up its own "independent" study of the scientific data, convinced the company to revise its proposal, and approved of the project when Al-Pac returned with a plan to cut emissions by a factor of five.

It was enough to make a cynic of almost anyone. When the Al-Pac license was awarded, a stand of sixteen aspen trees standing 15 meters (50 feet) tall cost the company Cdn.$90 in stumpage fees. Converting those same trees to pulp, the company made Cdn.$590; after finishing and paper processing in Japan, the end product was worth Cdn.$1250. Observed the Canadian Sierra Club's Elizabeth May: "Alberta's current political agenda is geared toward industry self-regulation. And what does that finally mean, in plain language? That decisions about whether Alberta's public forests are to be sustainably managed will be made in Japan." Judging from how Japanese companies were operating in the Canadian boreal forest, any prediction of "sustainable management" appeared to be optimistic, at best.

The Lubicon Cree and Diashowa-Marubeni: David and Goliath

It was one of the most successful boycotts in Canadian history. In 1998, eight years after the Japanese forest giant Daishowa-Marubeni International Ltd. announced its intention to log leased land from the Alberta government—land claimed by the

Lubicon Lake Indian Nation as unceded, traditional territory—
the company was backing down. After years of negative publicity
prompted by an international boycott that cost the company an
estimated Cdn.$14 million in lost revenue, Daishowa officials
confirmed that there would be no harvesting or purchasing of
timber from the area until the aboriginal land title issue was settled by the Alberta and the federal governments.

The destruction of Lubicon hunting grounds
from oil and gas development signaled the beginning
of a downward spiral for the band's
traditional way of life.

It was a long time coming for the Lubicon, who had stood by
helplessly as their traditional lands were turned into an industrial wasteland. Between 1979 and 1983, more than four hundred
oil wells were drilled within a 40-kilometer (25-mile) radius of
the traditional Lubicon community of Little Buffalo Lake. The
Lubicon were neither consulted about these developments nor
given a share of the profits. In 1988, the Alberta government sold
the rights to all the trees from the Lubicon's entire territory to
Daishowa—again without informing the Lubicon. In 1994, a sour
gas plant was established close to the settlement, in spite of Lubicon protests. (Sour gas is an impure form of gas that needs to be
treated to be usable. During this processing stage, concentrations
of gas impurities are released into the surrounding atmosphere,
causing damage to plant life and other parts of the ecosystem.)
Before long, hydrogen sulfide emissions from the plant were causing health problems in the Lubicon population, including still-
births, tuberculosis, respiratory problems, and cancer—at rates
that exceeded the national average.

The destruction of Lubicon hunting grounds from oil and gas

development signaled the beginning of a downward spiral for the band's traditional way of life. As more and more animal food sources disappeared from the bush, people stopped hunting and trapping and began to rely mostly on store-bought food. The loss of a way of life led to suicides and other social problems. As a result of the change in diet, the incidence of diabetes soared. A once thriving community was now hobbled by a 95 percent welfare rate, and 35 percent of the population suffered from the health problems already mentioned. The tragedy was summarized in a litany by Ontario Court justice James MacPherson, in his 1998 decision against Daishowa:

> The loss of hunting, trapping and gathering; the negative effect of industrial development on a communal spirituality rooted in nature; the disintegration of a social structure grounded in families led by successful hunters and trappers; alcoholism; serious community health problems such as tuberculosis; and poor relations with governments and corporate [entities] engaged in oil and gas and forest operations on land the Lubicon regard as theirs—all of these have contributed to a current state of affairs for the Lubicon Cree which deserves the adjectives "tragic," "desperate" and "intolerable."

The plight of the Lubicon might be unknown today were it not for the international boycott of Daishowa. In 1991, a newly formed group, the Toronto-based Friends of the Lubicon, launched a massive campaign in Canada and Europe to protest the company's violation of a 1988 agreement not to log the area until land claims were settled. The boycott focused on Daishowa packaging products, primarily paper bags produced for the Ontario retail and fast food market. By the mid-1990s, the campaign had spread to the United States; about fifty major companies from various parts of the world had joined the boycott. These companies included Woolworth's department store, the A&W fast food chain, Holt Renfrew, and the Body Shop, an ecofriendly chain of personal care boutiques. Activists in Washington State targeted customers of Daishowa's Port Angeles mill on the Olympic Peninsula, and there were plans to go after more high-profile corporate customers in the newspaper industry, such as the *Washington Post,* the *New York Post,* and *USA Today.*

In 1995, claiming that the boycott was costing the company U.S.\$3 million to \$5 million a year in lost sales—a drop in the bucket, given the company's annual profits—Daishowa filed a lawsuit against Friends of the Lubicon. The boycott, a spokesman said, was an "intentional interference with economic relations" and should be restrained by the courts. In 1996, Ontario's Divisional Court ruled in favor of Daishowa and prohibited Friends of the Lubicon from continuing its campaign to promote secondary boycotts of Daishowa's customers.

Buoyed by the ruling, Daishowa soon announced plans for a new Cdn.\$900-million paper mill, one of several new pulp-and-paper projects approved by the Alberta government. The proposed mill would use up to 15 percent of the pulp produced at its Peace River pulp mill to produce 300,000 tonnes of lightweight coated paper—the kind used in throwaway products such as magazines, flyers, and catalogs—annually for export around the world. The mill would convert eleven thousand trees a day into 1000 tonnes of pulp. In the words of one Lubicon supporter, the number of trees the mill would consume each year "would fill a woodlot the size of a football field to a height of 221 meters [725 feet]—the height of a 72-story skyscraper."

To jumpstart the project, the Alberta government agreed to supply Daishowa's paper mill with an additional 400,000 cubic meters (523,000 cubic yards) of wood from its existing Forest Management Agreement—a 12 percent increase in Daishowa's cut level—and charge the company 1989 level stumpage fees for the additional harvest. And that was just the warmup act. As well as the Daishowa mill, the government was looking at several other megaprojects for northwestern Alberta. In Grande Prairie, the Grande Alberta Paper Company had proposed a Cdn.$900-million paper mill; Ainsworth Lumber Company was opening a Cdn.$140-million panelboard plant, and Canadian Forest Products had begun a Cdn.$40-million expansion of its sawmill. In High Level, Alberta, Tolko Industries was constructing a Cdn. $103-million panelboard plant. Then there was the petroleum industry. Several oil company consortiums and corporate investors were planning to pump U.S.$25 billion into the mining of oil sands in northern Alberta—most of the plans including the 10,000 square kilometers (3900 square miles) of unceded Lubicon territory.

"The Lubicon cling to a lifeline of hope against great odds," wrote the Taiga Rescue Network's North American coordinator, Christopher Genovali. "Add this $900 million dollar Daishowa paper mill to its already built pulp mill, and Daishowa has all the timber rights to 4,000 square miles [about 10,000 square kilometers] of Lubicon Cree traditional territory. Add another $25 billion of oil sands development to the over 400 oil wells and a new sour gas plant, and one wonders how these people will survive with such devastating impacts bulldozed through their way of life."

For all their difficulties, however, it appeared that public opinion was on the Lubicon's side. At last, the industrial exploitation of Lubicon territory was giving both Daishowa and the Alberta government unwelcome attention in the international community. The Human Rights Committee of the United Nations found that the government's treatment of the Lubicon violated the International Covenant on Civil and Political Rights. The Sierra Club of the United States called Alberta the worst jurisdiction in North America for protecting the environment. And the *Multinational Monitor,* a monthly magazine focusing on issues of multinational corporate power (founded in 1980 by consumer advocate Ralph Nader), included Daishowa on its list of the Ten Worst Corporations of 1996.

Finally, on April 13, 1998, Friends of the Lubicon won back its right to boycott Daishowa. The consumer boycott not only was legal, ruled Justice James MacPherson, but was "a model of how such activities should be conducted in a democratic society." Dismissing Daishowa's claims for a permanent injunction, Justice MacPherson ruled that the plight of the Lubicon was "precisely the type of issue that should generate widespread public discussion." Because corporate rights to commercial expression were already protected by the Canadian Charter of Rights and Freedoms, he added, the same principle should apply to consumers.

But the victory was only a first step for the Lubicon, who had yet to negotiate their land claim with the federal government. In that struggle as well, the First Nations band had compromised; acceding to the federal government's colonial era land-claim formula, whereby an Indian band can claim only 2.6 square kilometers (1 square mile) for every five band members, the Lubicon are now seeking only 246 square kilometers (95 square miles) of the total area of 10,000 square kilometers (3900 square miles). They're also seeking Cdn.\$72 million for housing and services, Cdn.\$33 million to build local industry and agriculture, and Cdn.\$120 million in rent from the federal and provincial governments for forest and energy resources taken away from the land.

THE DRILLING FIELDS

Like the taiga of the Russian Far East, Alberta's woodlands are also a major source of oil and gas products. Alberta has always promoted the petroleum industry as its number one source of revenue. But many people associate this industry with the prairie flatlands: one of the most common scenes from Alberta Tourism is the procession of oil rigs that dot the horizon along provincial highways. But oil and gas exploration also cuts far into Alberta's boreal forest.

The numbers for oil and gas exploration in Alberta are staggering. By the late 1990s, 225,000 wells had been drilled, 1.5 million kilometers (almost 1 million miles) of seismic lines built, 750,000 kilometers (466,000 miles) of all-weather roads constructed, and 500,000 kilometers (310,000 miles) of pipeline right-of-way cut. According to some estimates, more soil has been excavated by one company, Syncrude, than from the construction of the Great Pyramid of Cheops, the Great Wall of China, the Suez Canal, and the ten largest dams in the world combined. In the early 1990s, the liquid waste created by Syncrude and another company near Fort McMurray, about 400 kilometers (250 miles) northeast of Edmonton, was said to pose an environmental threat worse than the *Exxon Valdez* disaster.

One of the most common scenes from Alberta Tourism is the procession of oil rigs that dot the horizon along provincial highways.

Viewed from an airplane, the forests north of Jasper National Park, stretching east to Saskatchewan and as far north as Yukon and the Northwest Territories, are no longer the carpet of green they once were. Like much of the Russian taiga, they're divided by a patchwork of seismic lines and access roads—the unfortunate product of more optimistic times. Between 1954 and 1993, a total of 6 million kilometers (3.7 million miles) of seismic lines was carved through the region's prairies, alpine grasslands, and forests. Some seismic lines in this region run for several kilometers in perfectly straight lines, intersecting with hundreds of other lines. As one forest expert put it recently, these lines are

like a sprawling road grid laid through the forest in preparation for the building of some giant city ... Canada's vast boreal forest may not yet look like Swiss cheese, but significant patches of it in Alberta, BC and Saskatchewan already do.

This patch of forest is part of an oil-rich region that stretches east into northern Saskatchewan and west into British Columbia. As in Alberta, the 1990s were a boom decade for the petroleum industry in northeastern British Columbia. In 1994–95 alone, more than 550 new wells were drilled, and the government made Cdn.$222 million in revenue from bids, fees, and rentals. Shortly afterward, an oil and gas consortium from Calgary, Alberta (Alliance Pipeline Ltd.), announced a plan to build a 3000-kilometer (1864-mile) high-pressure natural gas pipeline linking Fort St. John, British Columbia, and Chicago, Illinois. Supplying this pipeline would require massive drilling in the boreal forest of the Canadian Shield and Alaska—a prospect that would make the drilling of recent years "look like a picnic," as the Fort St. John chamber of commerce said.

It is in northern Alberta, however, that the biggest oil development scheme in the history of North America is now under way. Corporate oil investors are planning to pump Cdn.$25 billion over the next quarter century into the mining of the Alberta tar sands. Tar sands, also known as heavy oil sands, are crude oil deposits that are much heavier than most other crude oils. Formed by an infiltration of petroleum into porous sand near the earth's surface, this oil is often mixed with sand, limestone, or clay, and is separated from the enclosing rock with hot water or steam. Tar sands are becoming more prominent in the global marketplace as the cost of oil increases and supplies decrease. But chemically upgrading heavy crude oil into lighter crude oil is an expensive process, and not only for the companies involved: it takes two tonnes of sand to produce just one barrel of oil.

In Alberta, the area of tar sands to be mined includes four major northern regions—Athabasca, Cold Lake, Peace River, and

Wabasca—and covers a zone of boreal forest about as large as the province of New Brunswick. Under a new royalty regime recently announced by the province, companies will pay only 1 percent royalties on net profit until the companies pay off their capital investments.

The tar sands of Alberta are believed to contain approximately one-third of the world's oil resources. Some estimates put the area's recoverable oil reserve at one trillion barrels—equal to or greater than the reserves of Saudi Arabia. The oil industry claims that the tar sands reserves hold enough recoverable oil to supply Canada for a thousand years. By the year 2003, two of the five companies involved with the tar sands—Suncor and Syncrude— are expected to produce up to 550,000 barrels a day.

The tar sands of Alberta are believed to contain approximately one-third of the world's oil resources.

According to a June 1997 report by Environment Canada, the expansion of tar sands exploration is expected to affect more than 140,000 hectares (345,000 acres) of land, increasing the number of acid-rain–affected lakes fourfold. To put those numbers in perspective, Syncrude's operations alone will directly affect 15,000 hectares (37,000 acres) of land—or the equivalent of 25,000 football fields. Greenhouse gases from Syncrude gas emissions will increase 71 percent, and the survival of some 15,000 hectares (37,000 acres) of one of North America's best bird-breeding habitat will be put in jeopardy.

For every barrel of oil recovered from the tar sands, 2½ barrels of liquid waste are pumped into huge ponds. The massive Syncrude pond, which measures 22 kilometers (14 miles) in circumference, has 6 meters (20 feet) of murky water on top of a 40-meter-thick (130 feet) pudding of sand, silt, clay, and unrecovered oil. If a flood occurred, it would unsettle the sand dikes containing the lakes, contributing to a spill of toxic waste that could pollute the Athabasca River all the way to the Mackenzie Delta in the Northwest Territories.

As in Russia, the oil and gas developments of Alberta are a major contributor to global warming. Tar sands development releases more sulfur dioxide into the atmosphere than any other industrial activity in Alberta; the province itself emits 450,000 tonnes of sulfur dioxide annually. Petroleum operations in Alberta and northeastern British Columbia are the second largest source of sulfur emissions in North America, following the industrial regions of central Canada and the United States. All of this activity is dedicated to servicing fossil-fuel-burning automobiles, which warm our world and further imperil our forests.

CHAPTER 9

The Canadian Shield: Legislative Limbo Land

If you are a person before the law and Exxon or Ford is also a person, it is clear that the concept of democratic legitimacy lying with the individual has been mortally wounded.

—John Ralston Saul, *Reflections of a Siamese Twin*

One hundred and forty kilometers (87 miles) northeast of Winnipeg, not far from Manitoba's last year-round roadless wilderness area south of 50 degrees, is the oldest pulp-and-paper mill in the province. Built in 1925, it's a monument to the staying power of the logging industry. Just outside the mill gate is a logging truck with a feel-good slogan emblazoned on the side: Sharing Our Forests.

The irony of the slogan isn't lost on Garry Raven, the aboriginal trapper introduced in Chapter 2. Raven lives about an hour's drive north of Pine Falls on the Hollow Water reserve, whose mostly deciduous forests encompass the traditional lands of southeast Manitoba's Anishanaabe people. The Hollow Water band is one of four from this area whose impoverishment began shortly after the Pine Falls Paper Company moved in. So Raven —who is in his early fifties—has a lifetime of grievances against the company.

A Road Runs Through It

Since the 1930s, Pine Falls has earned huge profits from this land's resources, mostly at the expense of the Anishanaabe. When the mill first opened, half of its employees were supposed to be Native. But the aboriginal workers were gradually phased out—casualties, it was said, of poor training and lack of education. Over the years, the government has awarded timber licenses without consulting the Native community. At the same time, aboriginal people have lost control of their traditional trap lines—a key source of livelihood for countless generations of Anishanaabe people.

Having long ago accepted the presence of the forest industry as inevitable, the Anishanaabe people had hoped that their economy and traditional culture could coexist with industry in boreal harmony. There was the potential for employment and ecotourism, for example, in places such as the Bloodvein River—a designated Canadian Heritage site with at least three major canoe routes and several historical sites that could have been used for trap-line outings.

But the notion of peaceful coexistence between the Anishanaabe and the pulp-and-paper industry remained a dream. As the Pine Falls Paper Company consumed ever larger pieces of forest to feed its mill, there wasn't much hope for ecotourism, and the people's trap lines were disappearing amid the clear-cuts. The company's plans and license applications were mapped out behind closed doors, so local people were constantly left in the dark about how their community would be affected by the next logging project. In addition, businesses and infrastructures in the neighboring small towns appeared to have been designed to serve only the white communities employed directly by Pine Falls or other companies related to the forest industry and offered little or no opportunity for the area's Native population. The result is a legacy of mistrust and antipathy among the Native people toward those who are reaping the benefits of their traditional land and its forests. It's not that the aboriginal people were against logging—far from it. But they wanted some say in how the logging would be conducted. They envisioned a smaller-scale operation that would serve local needs rather than the massive removal of huge tracts of forest to supply the international market and increase the company's profits.

The notion of peaceful coexistence between the Anishanaabe and the pulp-and-paper industry remained a dream.

Moreover, a combination of mining operations, hydro dams, and Atomic Energy Canada's Pinawa storage lab for nuclear waste may have led to an outbreak of diabetes and skin rashes that didn't exist among the local Native population before industry moved in. Residents and scientists alike are convinced that such industrial developments—along with the introduction of a non-Native diet, junk food preservatives, and alcohol into Native culture—have played a role in causing these health problems. Toxic pollution, whether atomic, viral, or chemical, is known to affect the human immune system to the extent that many ailments, including allergic skin reactions, birth defects, and diseases such as cancer, can develop. This process occurs through a gradual accumulation of toxic wastes in the water supply and food chain. For many aboriginal people living a traditional way of life in the bush, where the surrounding plant and animal life provide a direct source of nourishment and untreated water is taken directly from neighboring streams, the resulting health problems may be slow to arrive, but they often have permanent effects. In the mid-1990s, an independent study by a Dalhousie University professor determined that cyanide leakage from dynamite used at the nearby Bissett gold mine had made its way into the local water supply. The damage caused by the Pine Falls Paper Company is more subtle and long term.

"They polluted our forest area by continually spraying without consulting us—herbicides and pesticides," says Raven. "And they damaged a lot of our wild harvesting that we do, wildlife that we eat. We used to eat porcupine—you can't even find porcupines now. And rabbits—they're just gone. [The company] told me they were going to come back in seven years. Well, that was twenty years ago and they haven't come back. When you're picking blueberries or medicinal plants, you see brown spots with holes in them. And I asked one time, 'What is that?' and they told me it's a combination of pesticides and acid rain. 'But acid rain comes from the city'—that's what I used to think."

When you're picking blueberries or medicinal plants,
you see brown spots with holes in them.

Things are much the same in nearby Sagkeeng, named for the lookout at the mouth of Winnipeg River, where the first European settlers arrived on Hudson's Bay Company ships. Sagkeeng is one of the largest Indian reserves in Manitoba, with some five thousand residents. As in many aboriginal communities in Canada, a good portion of its residents live on welfare and struggle to break free from alcohol abuse and their years in residential schools. Thanks in part to the contaminated water supply, cancer runs rampant here.

Anishanaabe elder Fabian Morriseau remembers what Sagkeeng was like before big industry moved in. Sitting in a roadside café over coffee and eggs one morning, he speaks of the silence he now hears in place of the frogs, ducks, and muskrats that used to populate the landscape. The hydro project eroded the land, putting hectares of territory under water where gardens used to be. The mining projects polluted the water, making the fish unsafe to eat. One day, an elder caught a fish and brought it to the university. "We were told it had cancer," recalls Morriseau, whose leathery face wrinkles into a scowl at the memory. "It had blisters all over it. Same thing with the rabbits. You don't bother to eat them. Some of us won't even eat the deer."

Ask people in Sagkeeng or Hollow Water how their problems began, and they all say that the logging roads ruined everything. "How did we lose our language?" Garry Raven's brother, Raymond, asks rhetorically. "When that road came in here. Of course, they [Pine Falls Paper Company representatives] didn't know our language—we had to understand theirs. When an all-weather road goes into an isolated community, you start losing your language. And that's what happened here."

The all-weather logging road has become a 20th-century metaphor for colonialism. Like the fur trade routes before it, the forest road promises much to the local people but delivers little. The loss of language is only the first step in the gradual attrition of native culture and identity that the road begins.

"When they built the highway," says Fabian Morriseau, "it sounded like a good idea. But we didn't know what it would bring." First, it brought welfare—the state dependency model of compensation for lost resources. Then it brought liquor stores, despite the community's vote to remain dry. One year twenty-four fatal car accidents took place in Sagkeeng, many of them caused by alcohol.

So when the Pine Falls Paper Company announced a two-year logging plan that would more than double its cutting rate—requiring a 337-kilometer (209-mile) all-weather road through the forest—the people were against it. The plan was never approved, but the company began building illegal bridges in the area. Garry and Raymond Raven counted at least sixty of them. "Just in our trap line alone, they plugged up the streams and spawning areas and blasted three areas at least where they were going to put bridges," says Garry. One of those explosions barely missed a wall of Native pictographs.

Where was government in all this? Regulatory activity has been token, at best. Although Pine Falls has been cited with violations under the federal Pulp and Paper Effluent Regulations, the company didn't even get a slap on the wrist for building illegal bridges. The federal government had the jurisdiction, under the Navigable Waters Protection Act, to fine the company for each illegal bridge built; instead, Pine Falls was retroactively awarded thirteen bridge permits.

In another bizarre development, the provincial government prohibited the Anishanaabe from entering one of their own sacred sites for fear that they would damage it. Long before the pulp mill was built, White Shell was a gathering place where people from neighboring communities held wild rice harvesting ceremonies each trapping season. But two decades ago the area was fenced off by the Manitoba government—apparently out of concern that snowmobiles were disturbing the petroglyphs. "They didn't consult the First Nations about this problem for us to arrive at a solution," says Morriseau. "Now we have to get permission to go into our own sacred land."

PASSING THE BUCK:
DEREGULATION IN THE FOREST

Such stories reflect the political power of the forest industry. Throughout the 1990s, as the G7 industrial nations and the International Monetary Fund began nudging the rest of the world toward a global economy, the role of the nation-state began to diminish faster than ever. Along the way, deregulation and the privatization of public services became the new gospel. The effect of these developments on the American school system and Canadian Medicare has been well documented in the media. But the effect on public forests is not so well known.

Throughout the boreal forest, government is getting out of the business of managing public forests. In Scandinavia, which has few state-owned forests left, that process is nearly complete. Russian forests, still reeling from the post-Communist hangover, are at the mercy of international speculators. Although Canadian forests are 96 percent publicly owned, no more than 23 percent of them are on federally controlled land. It is in the remaining 73 percent, owned by the provinces, where many of the current problems lie.

In Alberta, neoconservative premier Ralph Klein has slashed the budget for the provincial environment department while announcing that the oil industry will be responsible for monitoring its own emission levels in water and air. In other words, he is giving the oil industry the power to act as its own environmental watchdog. With billions of dollars at stake, few expect oil companies to conduct as thorough an assessment as the federal government. That's why there's so much concern about projects such as the Alberta Energy Company's New Express pipeline, which could threaten up to one hundred endangered species. Or Alberta's tar sands development, where the oil industry is proposing to recover some of the deeper oil reserves by injecting massive amounts of steam far into the ground. This method of extraction is said to require up to nine barrels of water for each barrel of oil recovered. No one really knows what the long-term effects of this method will be on the water table and the soil, but you can be sure that the results won't be highlighted in the average industry annual report.

As a result of deregulation, not even minimum standards are enforced. In British Columbia, the Ministry of Environment, Lands and Parks' northeast region—an area that covers 15.1 million hectares (37.3 million acres) or 62 percent of the entire land base of England—employs only three people at its Fort St. John headquarters to respond to all development proposals submitted by the oil and gas industry. Each year in this region, between 8000 and 10,000 kilometers (between 5000 and 6000 miles) of new seismic lines are cut, 300 to 500 new wells are drilled, and the Fort St. John office receives 3000 inquiries from industry—or 1000 for each staff member. Staff members are expected to respond to each inquiry within three to five working days. Not surprisingly, field time is almost nonexistent. Decisions are made by overworked bureaucrats who don't have the time to get away from their desks to see firsthand what possible risks might be posed by development. Thus, writes Ben Parfitt, "the oil and gas industry—with its $2.5 billion in capital projects in the north each year—goes about its business largely out of sight and rarely challenged."

This willingness of government to abdicate its traditional regulatory role is symptomatic of a recent upswing in neoconservative philosophy that depreciates the role of government in everyday life. In the late seventies, as an oil industry representative, Mike Robinson was required to work closely with senior Environment Canada bureaucrats. Now, as director of the Arctic Institute of North America, promoting comanagement agreements between industry and aboriginal communities, Robinson has witnessed a profound shift in the regulation of land use management; the watchdog role once assumed by government has been taken over by the private sector. "What's happened," he says, "has been a progressive understaffing of environmental regulatory agencies and departments to the point where now, corporations in many cases have been given the lead role for environmental regulation and monitoring. So, in essence, the fox is monitoring production in the henhouse."

Who, then, is looking after the long-term health of the forest? "As a citizen, I can't be the eyes and ears of the boreal forest monitoring industry," says Robinson. "As a citizen, I elect a government whom I expect will employ people who will do regulatory and stewardship tasks to protect the common good out in the bush. There's not enough of me out there to do that."

The Anishanaabe Triumph—For Now

When Garry Raven learned of the Pine Falls Paper Company's two-year plan—and then that the company was building illegal bridges on his trap line—he decided he'd had enough. "There was no consultation whatsoever with aboriginal people in the area," he recalls. "But in their two-year plan they said they consulted us. So we wrote letters to federal and provincial governments [saying] it never happened." Frustrated by the lack of initiative from their own tribal council, the Raven brothers developed the Anishanaabe Turtle Island Protectors with the help of Don Sullivan of Manitoba's Future Forest Alliance. Before long, the other three Anishanaabe bands from Black River, Broken Head, and Sagkeeng had joined the effort. Support also came from professional foresters, environmentalists, professors, and scientists from Australia, South Africa, Argentina, Mexico, Germany, and the United States. After a series of highly public protests, Pine Falls's two-year license application was withdrawn.

Sweet though the victory may be, however, Garry Raven knows it's only a first step. If the Anishanaabe people are to regain control of their land, the focus will have to shift to legislation. Down in Sagkeeng, Fabian Morriseau is trying to obtain a copy of the federal Treaty of 1871—now locked up and gathering dust in an Ottawa library—that he says entrenched aboriginal title to all resources in the area. Garry Raven, meanwhile, is focusing on federal statutes such as the Manitoba Natural Resources Transfer Act (1930). With that law, the federal government gave the province responsibility for dealing directly with First Nations. The provinces then transferred natural resources to industry. This transfer occurred without any consultation with First Nations—a historical injustice that Raven believes violated the Canadian Constitution. "The federal government gave [resource management] to the provinces and the province gave it to the industry," he says. "Even if we want a cord of [wood], we've got to go through Pine Falls Paper."

Raven wants to see the Natural Resources Transfer Act amended. "I think it will open up a lot of doors for a lot of aboriginal people, especially the ones that signed Treaty 5. Our agreement was for shared resources—whatever resources that any industry or any people that came here [took], they have to share with us. That's going to be a powerful document: they're going to go back to the original way where everything started."

A Bridge Too Far: Tolko Industries and the Canadian Environmental Assessment Act

Two days before visiting Garry Raven in Hollow Water, I was sitting in a fourth-floor hearing chamber at the federal court building in Winnipeg. Only a handful of law students and curious onlookers were present as the future of 11 million hectares (27 million acres) of public forest lands—and the credibility of the Canadian Environmental Assessment Act—hung in the balance.

Manitoba's Future Forest Alliance was taking the federal government to court. The reason? The Ministry of Environment had violated its own guidelines in failing to conduct a single environmental assessment on a forestry project that involved a chunk of federal and provincial park land bigger than all of New Brunswick and Prince Edward Island combined. At the center of the case was a forest management plan proposed by Tolko Industries. After buying its Manitoba operations from the forest giant Repap in August 1997, Tolko had inherited a thirteen-year plan that would create the largest forest management area in North America: a landscape divided by 860 kilometers (534 miles) of all-season roads. More than 2 million cubic meters (2.6 million cubic yards) of trees would be harvested annually.

Instead of recognizing the magnitude of this plan and calling for an independent expert assessment, the federal and provincial governments had continued the time-honored "piecemeal" approach of assessing each component of the forest giant's plan: one assessment for harvesting activities, another for a new mill, another for each new bridge proposal, and so on. This approach, argued the forest alliance, virtually guaranteed that the cumulative effects of Tolko's plan would not be discussed. These effects included the impact of the mill's effluent on fish, of logging on migratory bird habitats, and of roads on biodiversity and local

First Nations communities. So when the alliance's Don Sullivan learned that a federal assessment of the Sewap Creek bridge had been conducted the previous February, he called Rodney Northey, a 37-year-old Toronto lawyer specializing in environmental assessments, to initiate a lawsuit against Tolko and the federal Ministry of Environment.

Northey, who teaches environmental law at Ryerson University and previously worked for the Canadian International Development Agency, had already worked on five similar federal court judicial reviews. This one had the broadest implications for federal environmental law, because it included 11 million hectares (27 million acres) of land, a huge scale of forestry operation, additional mills, and huge infrastructure commitments. Despite this grand scale, the only part of the project for which Tolko sought federal approval was a single bridge. "If you're a bureaucrat," said Northey, "you receive an application for a bridge, you assess that bridge, you hand the application back, bridge approved, built. It's the simplest thing to do: no federal-provincial relations to worry about, no industry-federal government relations to worry about; it's a cinch. [But] it leaves out the real project. I mean, who the hell cares about a bridge? The bridge is the least significant thing going on with this project ... What we've been trying to show is, you've got to look at *all* the federal interests that are affected, not just the bridge."

Sullivan's lawsuit is predicated on the belief that by breaking up Tolko's land use plan into small components, the federal government is trivializing the cumulative effects on the land. Since the late 1980s, the assessment process has focused on the direct source of industrial activity—for example, emissions from treatment plants. But studies on biodiversity since then have shown that the encroaching infrastructure of roads can have the most significant ecological impact.

"There are going to be some enormous impacts as a result of having all-weather roads," Sullivan explains. "Everybody knows that once you've got a road, you've got all the other shit that comes with it: cottage developments, drugs, alcohol problems, you name it. Do you think aboriginals are truly going to participate in an economic sense in this development opportunity? I don't think so."

Tolko would require a very slippery lawyer indeed to convince a judge that bridges and access roads were not "related" to mills and harvesting operations.

Canadian law appears to include precedents for a court challenge. Section 15(3) of the Canadian Environmental Assessment Act (CEEA) requires that each CEEA assessment encompass every related undertaking proposed by the proponent. Tolko would require a very slippery lawyer indeed to convince a judge that bridges and access roads were not "related" to mills and harvesting operations. In 1990, the federal government did require an assessment of the entire project, then controlled by Repap. Two years later, a study by the federal Department of Fisheries and Oceans identified most of the 11-million-hectare (27-million-acre) land as "high risk" in its potential impact on fish habitats. And in 1995, then-federal environment minister Sergio Marchi reminded his provincial counterpart of the importance of the area. "Some species of neo-tropical migrant songbirds are known to breed almost exclusively within the Canadian southern boreal forest," Marchi wrote, in a letter to Manitoba environment minister Glen Cummings. "Other species have the most productive component of their range within these Canadian forests. Continent-wide consequences of potentially significant adverse effects to the populations of these birds and other wildlife are possible given the vast majority of their habitat is under forest management license and will be affected by forest operations."

Northey and Sullivan couldn't imagine a project sparking more federal interest than this one. If Ottawa still needed to be convinced that the piecemeal approach was flawed, it could always turn to Voisey Bay. In that case, the Newfoundland Court of Appeal rejected the piecemeal assessment approach for a smelter project. A similar assessment for a forestry project in Alberta had also been rejected by the courts.

If successful, the case against Tolko would turn the environmental assessment process on its head. A victory, muses Sullivan, would mean to Canadian forest protection standards what the spotted owl decision has meant to American standards. American legislators considered the spectrum of effects when they passed a law severely restricting logging within an 800-hectare (2000-acre) radius around known spotted owl nests. Which is why, says Northey, there is so much federal foot dragging in the Tolko case. "[Ottawa] is seeking to look like the good guys," he says. "There's a strong interest on the federal side—for those who aren't environmentally inclined—to have a very weak federal role to appease Quebec, and that's what we have here. The weakest possible federal role, to assess a bridge."

To make matters worse, the area in question was embroiled in a dispute about overlapping logging rights between Tolko and two other companies, Louisiana Pacific and Saskfor MacMillan, which had been granted logging licenses for a total of 2 million hectares (5 million acres). "It is unfortunate that Canadians must resort to the court system in their efforts to protect the environment," the Canadian Environmental Defence Fund wrote, in a *Toronto Star* op-ed piece. "While we would not expect the forest company to be concerned about preserving the integrity of the park areas, our government should be. After all, they created these parks."

Despite all these arguments, the case of Manitoba's Future Forest Alliance v. Tolko and the federal government was headed for defeat. On June 18, 1999, a Federal Court judge dismissed

Sullivan's effort to have a full environmental assessment of Tolko's logging plan—thus opening the door for development in a tract of boreal forest that covers more than one-fifth of the province. It was a major legal victory for the resource industry, and believed to be the largest single forestry concession in North American history. There would be no assessment of any part of the 11-million-hectare (27-million-acre) plan, other than a single bridge. There would be no environmental assessment of Tolko's logging plan. The boreal forests of jack pine and black spruce—slow-growing trees that often require more than a century to recover from logging, because the soil is thin and easily washed away—were now on the chopping block, along with the surrounding fish habitat and nesting area for millions of tropical birds.

As if to rub salt in the wound, Manitoba's Future Forest Alliance and the Canadian Environmental Defence Fund were ordered to pay Cdn.$85,000 in legal costs to Tolko and the federal government. Defence Fund lawyer Rod Northey couldn't hide his disgust. "It's like assessing the life cycle of a postage stamp while Lake Huron is being drained," he told the *Globe and Mail,* lamenting the federal government's narrow focus of environmental scrutiny. Back in November 1998, I had watched in the courtroom as Northey pulled out every supporting document he could find—several cases in which the courts had quashed a federal permit because of deficiences in the environmental reviews that approved them.

"We're now at the stage of being a royal commission," he had told me then, shortly after presenting his argument in court. "But do royal commissions get implemented anywhere? They get forgotten. The difficulty is, I agree, that at a certain stage you want to say, 'It's the effort that counts.' But unfortunately when we hit the stage where we are right now—in numerous sectors in Canada—it's not the fight that counts, it's winning that counts. *We need change.* Just simply to identify a problem—that's just one

more report to file, one more document lost in the shuffle."
Northey agreed that a 1992 assessment by the Department of
Fisheries and Oceans—in which industrial activity was said to
pose a "high risk" to surrounding wildlife habitat—was an "awe-
some" argument against Tolko's plan. But, he added, that assessment was now a forgotten document. "We're hauling it into
litigation, it should be [at] the forefront [for] every DFO official
making a decision in Manitoba, and yet you won't find any ref-
erence to it from them."

The case of Tolko's thirteen-year land use management plan in
Manitoba speaks volumes about the need for alternative development strategies for the boreal forest. The approach of government
and industry is simply to bring in a major capital producer such
as Repap/Tolko, grant the company access to a huge resource,
and then allow it to put the capital in place to send the resources
to market as quickly as possible, with the intention of creating
jobs while maximizing profits. Under this model, however, profits raised from resources in the boreal forest tend to disappear
to head offices in Vancouver, Toronto, or New York, rather than
benefiting local communities.

A much more effective model would recognize the different
needs of surrounding communities by reducing large-scale forestry in favor of local initiatives. In some parts of the boreal forest,
industry is already working with First Nations communities to
create jobs through small capital—an approach that accommo-
dates traditional forms of income such as hunting, fishing, and
trapping. By allowing economic activities other than large-scale
forestry to occur on a level playing field, says Sullivan, government and industry could create a dynamic economy based on
truly free-market principles—without having to strip-mine the
forest. "But we don't have a 'free market' principle here," Sullivan
concludes. "The forest industry is subsidized right to the hilt by
the federal and provincial governments."

Northey agrees: "It's a monopoly."

As the private sector becomes its own environmental watchdog, the problems that already existed in the boreal forest will only get worse. Yet the experiment continues in places such as Ontario, where the neoconservative government of Mike Harris has cut 40 percent of its natural resources department.

LANDS FOR LIFE: TILL DEATH DO US PART

When governments are forced to sell a difficult proposition to the public, they often resort to euphemism. In the marketplace, words such as "life" and "renewal" are positive concepts that advertising people use to inspire consumer confidence. When governments use these words, you can be sure they're a smoke screen for something else.

In Norway, a land use project called the Living Forest is promoted as a joint attempt by forest owners, industry, the Ministry of Agriculture, and a few environmental NGOs to arrive at a workable definition of "sustainable forestry." But other Norwegian NGOs claim that the project is dominated by industry and that conservationists have no role. This failing, they argue, compromises the integrity of the process itself; the twenty-three standards they have identified may be nothing more than an endorsement of current unsustainable forestry practices.

A similar skepticism surrounds an Ontario project called Lands for Life, an eighteen-month land management review launched in early 1997 whose purpose was to decide the fate of some 46 million hectares (114 million acres) of public lands, an area equal in size to Yukon. According to the Ontario government, the Lands for Life review was a "bold experiment in citizen participation," a model of democracy that would "help the government fulfil its commitment to complete Ontario's system of parks and protected areas." The treacly sentiment implied by the project's title suggested that the review would preserve "for life" the roughly 87 percent of Ontario that qualifies as Crown land.

Beyond the feel-good rhetoric of the public relations spin, however, the effect of Lands for Life was just the opposite. Far from preserving Crown lands, the project effectively wiped the slate clean for industrial interests, whose current access to the boreal forests of Ontario was by no means restricted. From the moment Lands for Life was announced by the Progressive Conservative government in February 1997, industry appeared to have the upper hand. The program's three goals were to "complete" Ontario's system of parks and protected areas, putting a freeze on any future parkland applications; to recognize the land use needs of resource-based tourism; and, over the next century, to ensure that the forest industry would have access to the landscape. Later, the government expanded the mandate to include increased access for mining and more opportunities for outdoor recreation, including hunting and fishing.

Many critics saw Lands for Life as an open tender process in which logging companies would compete to win hundred-year leases on huge chunks of Crown land. The forest industry was already on record as seeking compensable tenure *in perpetuity* across a majority of the land base. And, on territory not reserved as parkland, hundred-year leases were not out of the question. Even draft reports by the government advocated tenure in perpetuity. Conservationists were worried that even if such tenure agreements did not occur, the province would still lose important wilderness areas and wildlife species if the amount of protected territory was not significantly increased from its then 6.6 percent of the land base. Animal species such as the woodland caribou were already pushed northward by development, and greater numbers were disappearing each year. The eastern cougar and the wolverine had completely left the region. In some areas, there had been a 50 percent reduction in the moose population. Lake trout and brook trout populations were on the decline in all three regions, and rare tree species such as red and white pine were disappearing as well. According to predictions by the Toronto-based

Wildlands League, no area of land in the Great Lakes–St. Lawrence region greater than 5000 hectares (12,000 acres) would remain road-free after the next decade.

In April 1998, a report from the provincial environmental commissioner's office recommended that the Ministry of Natural Resources use a "precautionary principle" when establishing the extent and size of land designated to protect Ontario's natural heritage features. Two months later, the Lands for Life process kicked into gear. Three committees, representing Boreal West, Boreal East, and the Great Lakes–St. Lawrence regions, put everything from the Manitoba border east to Quebec and from Peterborough in the south to Hudson Bay in the north on the table. Of the 46 million hectares (114 million acres) up for review, 39 million hectares (96 million acres) were Crown lands.

From the very beginning, the three fourteen-member committees came under heavy fire for pro-industry bias. The conservation community was poorly represented at the roundtables, where the forest industry accounted for 51 percent of the seats. Forestry companies and the Ontario Forestry Association were lobbying the Ministry of Natural Resources to open the entire boreal system to business activity—including areas protected as parkland. One company, Buchanan Forest Products, told the Boreal West roundtable that "every hectare of forested land" in the northwest region, and "every tree on this land" would be required to run the company's sawmills.

"Lands for Life processes are not driven by any overarching ecological imperatives," concludes forest writer Ben Parfitt in his 1998 book *Forest Follies: Adventures and Misadventures in the Great Canadian Forest.* "They are first and foremost interest-based negotiations." Under the Lands for Life process, Ontarians in each of the three regions were presented with options in which logging was always a necessary component. Often, they were faced with the choice of saving only one of two woodlots within the same threatened ecosystem. The problem with Lands for Life and similar Protected Areas strategies, says Parfitt, is that they are based on the false and dangerous assumption that ecosystems can be divided into separate "special management zones" or "intense resource extraction zones" without affecting the overall health of each ecosystem. Conservationists object to this reasoning, if only because some parcels of land recommended for protection are too small to preserve habitat. Trees that grow along rivers and streams are especially vulnerable to nearby development.

Unemployment was 80 percent, and the community had lost 160 young people to suicide in the previous ten years.

In October 1998, shortly before the Lands for Life report was released, a number of northern Ontario Native bands threatened the government with legal action. They wanted some kind of guarantee that aboriginal communities would benefit from profits raised by the sale of resources. Native bands such as the Nishnawbe-Aski Nation had good reason to be wary of Lands for Life. Their treaty rights, signed in 1905, had largely been ignored by successive provincial governments. The band had 30,000 people living in fifty communities across the northernmost part of province, mostly under Third World conditions. Unemployment was 80 percent, and the community had lost 160 young people to suicide in the previous ten years. As Chief Charles Fox told the *Globe and Mail*, half of the band's communities didn't have water or sewer facilities—and some didn't have a telephone system. Fox, one of six chiefs to threaten legal, political, and civil disobedience campaigns, also threatened an American campaign similar to the 1995 publicity blitz that forced Hydro Quebec to drop plans for a new hydroelectric development in northern Quebec. Working with a broad coalition of American conservation and Native organizations—as the Lubicon example shows—can result in the kind of mass media exposure that embarrasses governments or industry into a change of course.

On October 30, the roundtable's consolidated Lands for Life report was finally released. Among its 242 recommendations:

- The amount of protected Crown land should rise only 1.6 percent, from 6.6 to 8.2 percent, and the remaining 92 percent should be made available to forestry and mining industries.
- Logging, mining, and mineral exploration should be permitted in conservation reserves.
- Deregulation of areas protected for natural heritage should be considered if existing mineral potential is found.
- Completion of a parks-and-protected-areas system using "floating reserves" should be considered. In such a system, certain sites would rotate between being protected and being used for extraction of resources.
- Lakes in parks should be managed to produce more fish for anglers.
- Habitat and game populations should be managed to "enhance" hunting opportunities in conservation reserves.

Given the scope of its decision—the government was charting the course for the next century of provincial forest policy—many were disappointed by the ministry stipulation of only thirty days for public response to the recommendations. "The document that people are being asked to look at contains about 240 recommendations, and some maps and charts," Ontario's environmental commissioner, Eva Ligeti, told a CBC radio host. "I think it's pretty ambitious for people to be able to comment on such a huge project in such a short period of time." Ligeti recommended a forty-five to sixty-day window of opportunity.

But the deadline remained. In the ensuing month, natural resources minister John Snobelen received 14,000 public submissions on the report—many of them hostile. People were especially concerned about the Forest Management Transition Team report that called for the logging industry to take control of forest management on Crown lands, with logging agreements of twenty years or more. Governments that chose to break the agreements would be forced to pay a fine. Many believed that a recommendation dealing with the disposal of Crown lands to promote "social and economic development" was just another plank in the Harris government's privatization agenda, which was well under way in the province's health care and education systems.

One petition, submitted by an ad hoc group of thirteen hundred scientists and academics, demanded that the protected area be increased to 20 percent—the minimum figure to preserve many species of animals, fish, and plants. "It is our opinion that to do anything less will lead to the further decline and loss of native habitats, wildlife species, and genetic resources that underpin the ecological integrity of a significant part of the Ontario and Canadian landscape," the group's public statement said. The 8.2 percent figure recommended in the Lands for Life report would "foreclose opportunities for recreational, cultural, spiritual and economic development on a truly sustainable basis."

This position was by no means radical. A growing number of Ontarians appeared to favor a strong conservation approach to the environment. One 1997 poll, conducted by Oracle Research, found that 82 percent of the population supported protection for the province's remaining wilderness area.

But the public will was hardly reflected by the Harris government's record on conservation issues. In October 1998, the Ontario Court of Appeal had affirmed an earlier ruling against the government for violating its Crown Forest Sustainability Act. (Authorities had failed to provide mature forest habitat for wildlife species including the American marten and one species of woodpecker.) And the next month, an Auditor General's report concluded that the provincial government had not consistently monitored wildlife populations, and had failed to

guarantee the continued good health of the province's fish and
wildlife resources.

By early 1999, public pressure was beginning to have an effect.
The Harris government—facing the end of its mandate—cited
widespread public support for its decision to increase the area of
protected Crown lands. While the final figure wouldn't come
close to the 20 percent recommended by the coalition of thirteen
hundred scientists, the province exceeded all expectations of the
Lands for Life process. On March 29, Mike Harris announced
that the government would save 12 percent of Ontario's Crown
lands from forestry, mining, and hydroelectric development. To
compensate foresters for the largest expansion of protected land
in the province's history, the government spent Cdn.$30 million
to help cover the loss of existing roads and bridges, build new
ones and develop new logging sites in the far north.

RECLAIMING THE FOREST

Like Chief Charles Fox and his Nishnawbe-Aski Nation in
Ontario, the Anishanaabe of Manitoba dream of a Lands for Life
forest policy that would truly respect the land and all the life in
it. In places such as Hollow Water and Sagkeeng, there's no
shortage of vision on how to get there. But first the aboriginal
people have to break the cycle of poverty that has kept them
down. Before that happens, says Garry Raven, the people have to
work together. Raven wants to establish a council of elders to rep-
resent the Anishanaabe people's interests. When that's done, he'd
like to establish an aboriginal interpretive center about the forest,
a place where visitors can learn about the traditional lifestyle of
the local aboriginal population and how it lives in the forest. A
joint venture between First Nations and industry, the project
would also include land use studies for the area. "We want our
aboriginal people to take people out into the woods and educate
them [about] what's out there and what we're trying to protect,"
says Raven. "Say, for instance, if you want to go to Shallow Lake,

the study will focus on Shallow Lake, and there will be an aboriginal person talking there in an aboriginal language, and she'll be talking about what's actually at Shallow Lake—what medicines are there, what types of fish are there, what pictographs are there, what canoes are there, what kind of trees are there, what kind of medical plants—you name it." So far, response from industry has been positive. "That's one of the things I told the paper mill they have to do, and they think it's a good thing," he says. "I told them, 'If we can build it that way and work together, it will be a model for all forests in the world.' They agreed."

Elsewhere in the boreal forest, ideas like Raven's were already beginning to bear fruit.

CHAPTER 10

Comanagement: A Bush-Made Solution

Only after the last tree has been cut down;
Only after the last river has been poisoned;
Only after the last fish has been caught;
Will you find that money cannot be eaten.

—Cree prophecy

In 1978, a thirty-five-year-old anthropologist from England arrived in northeastern British Columbia to begin a cultural odyssey on the remote Beaver Indian reserve. Hired by the government of Canada to study land use patterns in the region, the young, middle-class city boy with the large pickup truck caused quite a stir when he arrived on the reserve—where only one other functioning vehicle could be found. When he decided to leave the truck in town and get around on foot like everyone else, the locals were amused. "How are you going to eat?" they asked him. "What are you going to do now?"

Before arriving in this community, Hugh Brody had already published four books on aboriginal culture. He considered himself an expert on Native issues, having spent much of the 1970s working with the Inuit in the Arctic. At the Beaver reserve, however, Brody immersed himself in the traditional "bush" way of life as he never had before. Over the next year and a half, he accompanied his aboriginal hosts on fishing expeditions in the autumn, moose hunts in the winter, and beaver hunts in the spring. In doing so, he discovered an elaborate network of hunting trails and trap lines that had existed for generations. He learned about an economy that predated modern industry and agriculture, yet still thrived in the bush. And, as he watched an elder run a finger up and down a land use map—suddenly recalling a sacred site here, a log cabin there—Brody saw the flickering remnants of a disappearing culture come alive once again. The result of Brody's eighteen-month sojourn at the Beaver reserve was *Maps and Dreams,* a literary account of a people struggling to maintain their traditional way of life in the face of a major petroleum development. Nearly two decades after its release, the book is considered a minor classic. *Maps and Dreams* filled a vacuum in First Nations scholarship that had made an entire population invisible.

As he watched an elder run a finger up and down a land use map—suddenly recalling a sacred site here, a log cabin there—Brody saw the flickering remnants of a disappearing culture come alive once again.

Although the federal government had published studies in 1955 and 1967 on Indian life in Canada, neither of those studies mentioned the reserves located in the foothills, muskeg, boreal forests, and prairie between the northern Rocky Mountains and the Alberta and Yukon borders. But by 1978, there was growing concern that the Alaska Highway natural gas pipeline would cut directly through Indian lands and the Union of British Columbia Indian Chiefs was pressuring the federal government for a public inquiry. As a result, interest in the region was high.

Brody's journey through the bush revealed a vibrant, nomadic culture that had somehow managed to survive much longer than the southern world realized. The Indians' maps, wrote Brody, "demonstrate that the fur trade, gold rush, treaty signing, and trapline registration did not succeed in pushing the Indians off all of their lands." The problem by the end of the 1970s, however, was that none of those earlier developments matched the power or the economic influence of the timber, gas, oil, and mining industries now ripping through the forest. At the present rate of cutting and clearing, Brody predicted, all accessible timber in the entire region—mostly prime spruce—would be harvested within twenty years. Given this scenario, he wondered, how could an Indian economy possibly survive?

By exposing the real threat of industrial development to the traditional Native way of life, *Maps and Dreams* helped the Indians of northeastern British Columbia establish their treaty rights to hunting, fishing, and gathering on traditional land. At the same time, Brody's inclusion of traditional land use maps—which included data on everything from historical hunting and trapping routes, the location of old cabins, and even the exact places where certain animal populations could be found—uncovered for its southern readers a previously unknown world. Traditional environmental knowledge and aboriginal wildlife management, systems based on thousands of years of wisdom, were still being used by Native people in the late twentieth century.

HOMEMADE SOLUTIONS FOR THE BUSH

Although *Maps and Dreams* continues to be valued as a work of history and literature, the traditional land use study described in Brody's book was just a beginning. In the early 1980s, much more work was needed to develop a methodology for land use research that included the entire community in the research. There needed to be a way of developing archives for each aboriginal community so that information remained in the community after the project was completed. And there needed to be a way for aboriginal groups to retain the copyright of any written material produced by and for the community.

For an increasing number of Native groups in the North, that way is being found in comanagement, a method of sharing control and management of resources among local communities, industry, and regulatory agencies. Comanagement combines the rational inquiry of modern science with the qualitative discourse of traditional knowledge and aboriginal wisdom. A uniquely boreal solution, it also points the way to more sustainable land management and settlement of disputes in temperate and tropical rain forests.

Comanagement is by no means a new idea, but it has evolved over the decades. The concept dates back as far as the late 1800s, when Greenland established a harvesting registration process for the polar bear. (Since the birth of home rule government in 1979, however, indigenous communities and government have fought over hunting issues.) In North America, the Northwest Territories was the first boreal region to experiment with comanagement when local hunters and trappers from Aklavik met with the government in 1942 to discuss managing their resources. In 1946, the first hunters-and-trappers committee was formed in Fort Smith. But comanagement has only fifteen years of legislated application in northern Canada. The current model for this concept is based on comprehensive land claim settlements reached by the Department of Indian and Northern Development with the Inuvialuit (1984), Gwich'in (1992), Sahtu (1994), and Nunavut (1995).

Comanagement offers a cooperative model of land use that represents the true spirit and intent of previously signed treaties, as First Nations elders understood them. By following the principles of comanagement, it is quite possible for indigenous communities, government, and industry to agree on how a particular parcel of land and its resources are to be managed. At the Arctic Institute of North America, Mike Robinson and his associates have developed a comanagement model that combines three important elements.

- *Traditional Environmental Knowledge.* A form of wisdom unique to aboriginal people, this knowledge is based on lived experience passed down through generations and involves a deep understanding of the natural world and how to live within it.

As described in Chapter 2, the bush economy of First Nations culture is based on the cumulative wisdom of the hunting, gathering, and extended-family nomadic bands that predate sedentary living. Agricultural societies were based on what the great American naturalist Aldo Leopold once referred to as an Abrahamic relationship to the earth: a hierarchical system, based on the Book of Genesis, in which God had dominion over the land and all its life-forms. Many logging, gas, oil, and mining executives continue to be governed exclusively by such Abrahamic assumptions.

Traditional environmental knowledge is cumulative. It is also transmitted orally. And it is the basis of stewardship in the bush economy. Comanagement requires government and industry to understand that science—the rational mode of thought—is not the only means of making decisions about land use.

- *Traditional Land Use and Occupancy Studies.* In this lengthy process, maps are drawn, stories gathered, and fixed data recorded that confirm an aboriginal community's historical presence in a certain landscape.

There are several good reasons for an aboriginal community to conduct a land use and occupancy study of its traditional territory. Aside from recording and illustrating the people's continuing presence in one area, the study serves as a living document, passing on traditional environmental knowledge to younger generations in writing; elders formerly transmitted this knowledge through oral storytelling. The study can be used both as a historical record for the community and as an educational tool for nonaboriginal people.

For example, these studies can teach southern readers the importance of the fur industry to some boreal communities.

Many southern-based conservation groups oppose all hunting of fur-bearing animals without realizing that many aboriginal communities depend on the fur industry for their
livelihood. A land use study can increase traditional uses of
the land for the current generation by teaching young people
how the bush economy worked in earlier times. At the same
time, the land use study is a powerful expression of a community's knowledge of itself. Any aboriginal group with its
own study has much more leverage and bargaining power
than a group without such a study when entering into
comanagement negotiations with government and industry.

• *Participatory Action Research.* This method of information
gathering compiles the research for land use studies. It is
highly democratic, involving the entire community in the
process of selecting which information should be sought,
how the research ought to be conducted, and how the results
will be recorded and presented.

When Mike Robinson arrived at the Arctic Institute of
North America in 1986, there was a growing consensus that
the old model of scientific research did not serve northern
communities well. Although people appreciated the few training and employment opportunities the oil companies offered
(to say nothing of the belt buckles, toques, chewing gum,
and big bass drums for the school band emblazoned with the
corporate logo), there was a growing resentment of the lack
of community commitment displayed by visiting researchers.

In the old model, a group of well-paid white men from
the south traveled north in the summer when the weather
was good, studied only the subjects that interested them
(rather than addressing local concerns), and then—without
establishing any connection to the community—packed
their bags and left before the weather got cold. Then there
was the alienating use of language. Biologists visiting northern communities addressed groups of aboriginal people in

English only, and their tendency to use techno-speak compounded the difficulty for Native listeners. One biologist aware of this tendency thought he was being helpful by bringing a boxful of whistles to a public meeting in northern Alberta. Encouraging his aboriginal audience members to give him a toot whenever he said something incomprehensible, the hapless professor got the message soon enough. For the first hour of the meeting, the whistle blowing was almost continuous. With participatory action research, there's no need for a whistle because local people can do their own research, in their own language, about their own land.

Twelve years after Robinson's arrival, the Arctic Institute of North America has become a world leader in recognizing the crucial role that local wisdom plays in the overall management of lands and resources. Although not strictly an advocacy organization, the Arctic Institute is one of the first research centers to combine scientific inquiry with the traditional knowledge of First Nations culture. The success of its mandate—to conduct traditional land use studies that then lead to comanagement regimes for northern aboriginal communities, government, and business—can also be seen in the bottom line. By 1998, the institute boasted Cdn.$1.5 million in revenues and a Cdn.$2 million annual budget for research and publication.

THE DENE THA' LAND USE STUDY: A PAST MADE VISIBLE

One of the biggest obstacles to comanagement has been a legacy of unresolved land claims. Treaty No. 8, which covers northeastern British Columbia, the northern half of Alberta, and a small pocket of northwest Saskatchewan, officially ceded traditional Native lands to the government of Canada. But many of the Native communities subject to the treaty believe they were betrayed by the process.

Perhaps the best known among these people were the Dene Tha'
First Nation, an Athapaskan-speaking people from the Bushe
River, Meander River, and Chateh communities of northwest
Alberta. By 1996, there were about 2200 Dene Tha' residing here,
the largest group settled in Chateh. The Dene's traditional territory, however, extends into northeastern British Columbia and
parts of the southern Northwest Territories. Until this century, the
Dene Tha' lived a nomadic lifestyle, constantly traveling in search
of food and water. Like their ancestors thousands of years before,
the Dene lived everywhere on their traditional land, burying the
dead wherever they traveled and using every animal for subsistence.

In 1900, the Dene Tha' were among several Native populations
to sign Treaty No. 8. The Dene leadership had no idea what they
were signing because the treaty was written only in English and
the aboriginal interpreter, Louis Cardinal, spoke only Cree.
Treaty No. 8 effectively reduced the Dene's "owned" territory
from several thousand square kilometers of traditional lands
covering the southern Northwest Territories, northeastern British
Columbia, and northwestern Alberta to a tiny pocket near
Chateh, where they live today. It also removed all their rights to
manage land outside the reserve base. One hundred years have
obscured the details of what exactly was said during the negotiations, but the Dene's understanding of the spirit and intent of the
treaty is miles from Ottawa's perception, which was that the
Dene had voluntarily given up all their rights to land use management outside the reserve. According to the elders, the treaty
was supposed to involve a "partnership" with the government over
stewardship of the land. They thought the treaty commissioners
had accepted the Dene's use of words such as "co-existence" and
"protecting the land for future generations." The Dene saw Treaty
No. 8 as a "peace treaty" that would allow aboriginals and non-
aboriginals to live side by side; under this arrangement, the Dene
would continue hunting and trapping on all their traditional territory, not just the reserve land.

"My grandfather was the one who signed the treaty," Alphonse Scha-Sees told researchers during a land use study project. "At that time, my grandfather stated that on the condition that they will forever help and work with each other—the Dene Tha' and the government—the treaty would stand. On that basis, he signed. In this spirit, he signed."

Historians can speculate forever on what happened between the writing of the commissioner's report and the approval of the final draft for Treaty No. 8. But it's possible that the Dene leaders were hoodwinked by a federal government eager to open up the West for development while avoiding the violence that occurred in the fight for the American frontier. Whatever the case, the Dene have had to live with the consequences ever since.

LIVING WITH DEVELOPMENT

The Dene were one of the last aboriginal peoples in North America to experience the full-scale encroachment of modern industry. It wasn't until the 1950s that missionaries, traders, and government bureaucrats made their first major contact with this part of northwestern Alberta. The nomadic lifestyle of the Dene began to disappear when the first Catholic residential school in Chateh opened in 1951. Children had to live at the Assumption School, away from their families, for ten months of the year. So their families simply picked up and moved closer to town to be near them. Since 1962, when the massive flooding of Hay Lake destroyed the nearby settlement of Habay, the majority of Dene people have moved to Chateh to live in permanent homes.

Despite the presence of police and nursing stations, a gas station, a grocery store, and a courthouse, the Dene Tha' managed to maintain their traditional lifestyle in the bush economy. Moose and duck—staples in the Dene diet—continued to be plentiful. Lakes filled with muskrat and beaver abounded. And everyone still spoke the Dene language. But with the arrival of oil and logging industries in the 1960s, things began to change.

Dene Tha' elder Alphonse Scha-Sees recalled having seventy lakes on his trap line alone. But now there are no lakes—several decades of clear-cut logging and deep-pit mining drained much of the water away. At the same time, oil and gas activity cut through the forests, removing trap lines and forcing many fur-bearing animals away from the area. These developments, which occurred over several decades, gradually sucked the lifeblood out of the Dene bush economy. Before industry, the church, and small-town infrastructure moved in, the community worked in a cooperative spirit, sharing the land and its resources because nobody "owned" them as private property. But the industry presence gradually shifted that community spirit until it began to disappear. Instead of living in the bush in tents, people now lived in the village in private houses. Instead of getting their food from the forest, they got it from the local store. Before, neighbors would check on each other, or inquire about a sick relative. Now, people were disconnected. "Long ago, people used to give each other flour and moose meat," recalled Emma Metchooyeah. "People used to help each other out back then. Today it isn't like that. Nowadays you have to buy everything."

In the Dene's traditional territory alone, there were more than twelve thousand well sites by the mid-1990s. Logging activity had severely altered habitat for fur-bearing animals, and seismic lines and oil and gas installations crossed every trap line. "Our people need to be out on the land," Charlie Chissakay told land use study researchers, "but the industrial activity makes it impossible."

The Dene Tha' land use project sponsored by the Arctic Institute of North America began in November 1995 with a meeting held in Chateh. The meeting was attended by Dene leaders and sponsoring representatives from the Arctic Institute, various levels of government, and industry. By January 1996, three researchers had been chosen from the community and the project was up and running.

Phase I of a traditional land use study typifies the approach used in participatory action research. It begins when a small group of community residents is trained to interview elders, hunters, and trappers who have participated in the bush economy. The purpose is to establish some historical patterns of land use. Interviews with elders are recorded on tape, and information is recorded on maps covering the traditional territory. In the Dene Tha' project, researchers agreed not to put time limits on the interviews or to set rigid guidelines for subject matter, because in some cases there would only be one opportunity for an interview. Some elders were in frail health, but others were difficult to schedule because they needed to be convinced that the project would serve community needs. By allowing for this "open-ended" style—which allowed elders to expand on their experiences and retrieve long-forgotten memories—the process showed respect for elder wisdom.

Interviews were held in Dene kitchens and living rooms, sometimes while children played around them, and in the Dene band office in Chateh. Maps were brought to community meetings to verify information and make sure that all areas of interest were included in the study.

Researchers were looking for two kinds of information. The first kind was "fixed site data," which included specific place names, trails, camps, cabins, settlement sites, migration routes, graves, spiritual and historical sites, and important hunting and trapping areas in the territory. Medicine gathering places were not included, because, as one interview subject put it, "Any person cannot just pick ground medicine. It is dangerous if one does not know how to use it." The second kind of information was ethnographic: traditional wisdom passed on through the generations.

The maps provided crucial evidence of the history of these communities. Before the land use study, communities such as the Dene Tha' had no way of telling resource companies how their activities were harming the Dene's traditional areas. Beginning with a Macintosh computer, the research team created a base map including all the lakes, cabins, and trails in the area. This map was followed by another for graves and historical sites, and then another for hunting and trapping areas, locations of fur and big game, and so on. Tiny stickers representing each one of these categories, or icons, were placed on the map wherever the elders determined that the category (for example, locations of moose, grave sites) existed on the real landscape.

During Phase II of a land use study, the information is digitized from hard copy maps to the computer-based Geographic Information System (GIS). In many cases, the fixed site data are verified by a Global Positioning System (GPS), which scans the site and determines the exact locations of each icon labeled on the hard-copy map. Global Positioning Systems are fairly inexpensive, hand-held computerized units that calculate the precise coordinates of any location on a land surface within 10 meters (32 feet) or less of the target location. The GPS sends a beam to a number of earth-orbit satellites, which then determine the target location. The data are stored on the GPS memory and then downloaded to the GIS, which enables the user to create a map and locate on that map the coordinates frozen in time by the GPS.

During this phase of the Dene Tha' study, from May to September 1996, Dene researcher Adrian Tecomba was taken on long field trips into the bush accompanied by elders, hunters, and trappers. He spent many nights seeing places his grandfather had told him about—including, for the first time, his great-grandparents' graves.

The publication of the elders' stories breathed new life and pride into the traditional bush way of life and inspired many of the Dene Tha' young people to learn more about their culture. Among the interviews:

- Seventy-two-year-old Louison Ahkimnatchie described an eagle's nest near Twig River that had been there since he was sixteen years old.

- Emma Metchooyeah described how people were buried in coffins made of giant spruce trunks cut in half: "People buried long ago were wearing all white, lying down. You would oversize the coffin and put it together, and dress the person good. Then after, you put the person in white and sew them all together. You put the feet together and wrap it up good up to the head, cover and all. That is what I saw."
- Seventy-four-year-old Adam Solopree described how moose urine kept him alive as an infant. Both of Solopree's parents had died—his mother after falling into the lake and getting caught in a fishing net, and his father in his sleep soon afterward. "For three days I did not have breast milk," he said. "My foster parent took me home and my step-father went hunting for moose. He killed a moose and took out the bladder sac from it and made a hole in it and that is how they fed me."
- Mary Beaulieu described some of the Dene medicine plants of Rainbow Lake. Remedies for sores, rashes, and common colds are called mouse droppings, she says. "If you cook it with lard, it turns black. It doesn't take two dressings to heal the open sore. On the side of the highway around the spring, there is some medicine for chest pain, such as tuberculosis. It looks like potatoes at the root, but one cannot play with it; it is very powerful."

At some point before the final report is published (Phase III), the land use study goes through the validation process. This step is the crucial meeting when all the elders and current hunters and trappers who have been interviewed are invited to review the maps for any mistakes. They are also asked to provide names of new species or other relevant information. By the end of the meeting, everyone is satisfied that the map as fixed is accurate.

Participatory action research methodology ensures that the copyright of the document remains with the community. Because there is no single writer for the project, the author is simply listed as "study team." While scientists require peer review for their published work, the land use study is validated by a thank-you letter from the band chief.

Reindeer Herding in Murmansk: Perestroika for the Sámi

Initiated in 1995 by the Arctic Institute, the Russian Kola Sámi Association, and the Russian Academy of Sciences, the Russian Sámi Comanagement Project was established to monitor the effects of oil and gas development on the Sámi population in a region and economic system in the advanced stages of collapse. Since the disintegration of the Soviet system, Russia's two thousand Sámi have suffered from the loss of state-sponsored health care, pensions, employment on farms, housing, and most other forms of support the Soviet system once supplied. In the free-market system, the Sámi have been left to fend for themselves on a landscape littered with "aging mines and smelters; atomic power stations; missile, submarine and surface fleet bases; and three reported atomic waste storehouses." Despite their plentiful numbers right now (the reindeer population has hovered at about sixty thousand for at least a hundred years), reindeer could be threatened by poaching if the Russian economy doesn't turn around and more job opportunities become available. One herder interviewed for the project was nearly shot by poachers blazing through his herd on snowmobiles.

Although fewer than one hundred Sámi were still herders by the mid-1990s, reindeer herding continued to have major cultural significance for the larger population; the Sámi year still honors the seasonal cycle dictated by herding, and the reindeer continues to be a metaphor for Sámi spirituality. According to ancient myth, the nature of the Sámi soul was determined by the fate of three Sámi daughters. One married a seal, the second a raven, and the third a reindeer. The reindeer proved to be the best husband because he treated his wife well, worked hard, and practiced cleanliness. That is why, as the authors of *Sami Potatoes* put it, "the most spiritually pure Sámi existence is living out on the tundra with the reindeer." Or, as the Sámi themselves like to say, "What's good for the reindeer is good for the Sámi."

One herder interviewed for the project was nearly shot by poachers blazing through his herd on snowmobiles.

Sadly, the twentieth century has been good for neither. During the 1920s, the new Soviet state imposed a policy of compulsory reindeer harvests; Sámi were ordered to kill reindeer for the use of the Russians. In 1928, reindeer and Sámi property were collectivized in the village of Voron'e. Those who resisted were killed or exiled. A second wave of collectivization from 1933 to 1941 launched a period of cultural genocide as the Sámi lost their rights to land, water, and their nomadic way of life. All Sámi lands were proclaimed the property of the Soviet Union. In several Sámi villages, all the men were executed and the women and children were sent to labour camps or left to fend for themselves after being kicked out of their homes.

The collectivization phase coincided with massive industrialization on the Kola Peninsula. As new towns cropped up to support government service centers, military bases, and mining or smelting operations, the Sámi became the people the 20th century forgot. In 1933, the population was 1800. Today's population of two thousand is only 0.16 percent of the one million people living in the Kola region. The largest river in the region is now off-limits to Sámi fishers, and there are no small businesses to compete with larger operators. Thus, traditional forms of livelihood, such as reindeer herding, fishing, and hunting, offer the only hope of survival for a culture weakened by unemployment and alcoholism. That the Sámi have survived at all is amazing, given all they've endured.

The comanagement project was funded by a Cdn.$100,000 grant from the Gorbachev Foundation, a creation of the former Soviet leader and the University of Calgary "dedicated to easing the economic and social transitions occurring in Russian society through joint Canadian/Russian research initiatives." One of the foundation's first projects, it required a five-member project team: three Sámi, a member of parliament for Murmansk, and an anthropologist from Moscow.

There were some obstacles to overcome. The Kola Sámi Association was not considered an official organization by the Murmansk Duma. Nor was the Sámi homeland on the tundra legally recognized. These challenges were compounded by overlapping jurisdictional requirements. In addition to the federal duma and the provincial, or oblast, duma, there were municipalities and military zones, which had their own regulations. Thus, a research team monitoring the annual migration of reindeer from the boreal forest to the Barents Sea coast could, at any given time, be crossing federal, oblast, municipal or military, or Sámi zones of influence. As Mike Robinson has said, "When you create a comanagement regime, you'd better make damn sure that you have all of the regulatory authorities at the table."

The comanagement team also faced political obstacles in the use of its standard equipment. Even in post–Cold War Russia, the use of a GPS instrument linked to American satellites would be highly inappropriate. Russia remains one of the most militarized zones in the world. Many scientists have had such equipment confiscated upon entering the country because GPS instruments are considered useful surveillance and espionage technology. Thus, the use of such equipment can jeopardize a community and, says Robinson, "make our work in Russia difficult, if not impossible."

Furthermore, there are cultural limitations to North American methodology. The mapping of traditional knowledge by hand or

GIS equipment cannot fully capture its anthropological significance. The project team based its activities on four principles of appropriateness:

- technical efficiency (not being wasteful)
- economic efficiency (using locally available materials)
- environmental compatibility
- social and cultural compatibility

In the end, each map was validated by local Sámi elders and reindeer herders in public, open-house sessions where researchers stood by their work to make corrections and add new data. In addition to the Kola Sámi Association, the project was endorsed by the mayor of Lovozero, where most of the research took place, and the vice-governor of Murmansk County.

According to Mike Robinson, the project has created a basis for land use reform and protective stewardship for the sixty thousand reindeer that remain in nine brigade units organized under the Soviet system. For the first time on the Kola Peninsula, land use and occupancy maps have set a foundation for a new Murmansk County system of development project review and approval.

Nontimber Forest Products

Other comanagement agreements in Russia include the marketing of nontimber forest products. In the Altai Republic, a group of small businesses, environmental groups, and scientists has joined to form the independent Association for the Use of Non-Timber Forest Products. The association is helping to plan marketing and business strategies to support the growth of a nontimber forest products industry.

A number of these projects are already under way in the Russian Far East. Not far from the Bikin River, the indigenous people of Krasnyy Yar village have developed a comanagement proposal for gathering, processing, and marketing the more than two hundred medicinal plants found in the forest. Near the village of Katen, Kafensky Forest Management Enterprises—a business venture of two former employees of Lespromkhoz, a state-owned company notorious for its bad logging practices—is seeking markets for the honey and ginseng that surround the area. (At the same time, Kafensky is proposing that local sawmills and a furniture factory be built to generate jobs for the villagers and increase the added value of the timber.)

The Duty to Consult

One obstacle to comanagement agreements for most of this century was the failure of federal and provincial authorities to consult with aboriginal communities about industrial developments that affect Native communities. Governments have a legal duty to consult First Nations people about such matters, but it's only in recent years that the court system has compelled them to do so. A series of Supreme Court of Canada decisions concerning Section 35(1) of the 1982 Constitution Act has raised new questions about treaty and aboriginal rights and how governments have violated them. *Delgamuukw v. British Columbia* (1997), for example, determined that governments have a fiduciary duty requiring that "consultation must be in good faith, and with the intention of substantially addressing the concerns of Aboriginal peoples whose lands [or other rights] are at issue."

That description of consultation is in stark contrast to the type of consultation that often occurs in practice. In a recent paper co-written with University of Calgary colleagues Monique M. Ross and Cheryl Sharvit, Mike Robinson used a fictional consultation story based on real-life examples to illustrate some of the complexities and conflicts that can arise over differing interpretations of rights and obligations under the law.

In the story, "Dave" the forest engineer goes to visit "Miles" the First Nations resource referral officer at the Native band office. The purpose of the meeting, in Dave's view, is to show Miles his company's plan for a new development project—thereby fulfilling what he believes is the extent of his consultation duty. Miles has agreed to the meeting because his band needs all the information it can get about future development projects. Given these two perceptions, both parties make many assumptions based on their own cultural views. The following is an adapted version of "A Consultation Story."

> Dave, arriving at the office in a brand new company-owned 4×4 pickup truck, sits down in the waiting room. Miles can't meet him just yet, because he's tied up on the phone after spending most of the morning with officials from six oil and gas companies, a forest company rep, and some bureaucrats from the Department of Indian Affairs and Northern Development.
>
> Miles had come away from those meetings with a pile of cerlox-bound reports, binders full of data he'll never have time to read, and formal letters requesting various actions. He's still recovering from the previous week's forestry conference in Edmonton and yesterday's long drive back from Calgary, where he attended a training session for the Geographic Information System used for traditional land use studies. Dave is just one of several challenges Miles's band will have to face in the coming months.
>
> When the two men finally meet, Dave passes Miles a binder outlining his company's cutting plans for the next five years. Miles puts it on his desk with twelve other binders. Miles is soft-spoken and doesn't know how to deal with the fast-talking, results-oriented Dave, who wants to know how soon Miles can complete his review. Dave asks a whole bunch of direct questions that Miles finds intrusive, since the two men don't even know each other. Miles changes the subject and talks about the weather. Dave, puzzled by this behavior, repeats the question: "Can you tell me how your

team does its review?" Dave secretly resents the necessity of meeting with Miles, because his company's Forest Management Agreement with the province doesn't say anything about a "resource referral process review." The company wasn't even cutting the band's timber, so what were the Natives complaining about? The 1899 treaty was between the band and the federal government, so it should have had no effect on his company's operations. Not sharing any of these thoughts with Miles, Dave tells the aboriginal man he'd like to see his consultation comments by the following week.

Miles, not knowing what else to say—or even what the two of them are achieving with this meeting—reluctantly agrees to Dave's deadline. When the two men part, Dave thanks Miles for a "really good meeting" and heads off to visit the oil and gas producer's office. Miles opens the binders and, seeing words like "boreal," "ecosystem management," "berm area," "riparian," and "plantation softwood," closes them again and places them on top of his metal bookcase— next to another pile of reports. Dave, relieved to be driving away from the band office, is convinced that his next meeting will be more "professional." Miles, whose job depends on funding from the band council (which had denied his request the previous year for more staff members to handle the huge volume in resource referrals) feels somewhat defeated and wonders how the band council and his father, a trapper, will react to the news of this "deadline."

The authors are quick to remind the reader that not all resource companies conduct their consultations in such a shoddy, disrespectful manner. Many logging and mineral companies make a genuine effort to consult with aboriginal communities. But the story of Dave and Miles reflects some of the problems that can occur in a consultative process where there is no government representative present, no guidance to either industry or the

First Nation about the rights and responsibilities of each party, and no awareness of the legal standard against which their consultation should be measured. In such a vacuum, the distance separating the two men's cultural world views (Dave's rational-planning model of sustained-yield curves based on forest ecology and the species dynamics of each particular forest stand versus Miles's qualitative-wisdom model based on traditional knowledge and spiritual values) grows even wider.

If the logging in this fictional case were to proceed, or if the band council sought an injunction or claimed an infringement of treaty rights, the government would likely argue that the contact between Miles and Dave fulfilled all the company's obligations to consult, even though government was nowhere to be found during the meeting. "Because the government and/or company and the Band have no comanagement agreement, and the province gives primacy to the Forest Management Agreement," the authors conclude, "there is no legal context other than treaty rights for consultation to occur." Until treaty rights are recognized and put into action by government, they only exist in the abstract. In other words, government involvement is crucial to the process.

COMANAGEMENT AND TREATIES: FOLLOWING THE COURT'S LEAD

In Canada, some of the more successful comanagement agreements have occurred where land claim settlements or other treaties are in place. Not surprisingly, such agreements have often taken place in areas—including parts of the Northwest Territories and Yukon—where the resolution of land claims earlier this century was achieved before industry became a major presence. The rules of land use management, in other words, were clear before development began. The Gwich'in, the Inuvialuit, and the Nunavut all settled their comprehensive claims before the arrival of large-scale industry.

Apart from the comprehensive land claims of the James Bay

Cree (1978) in Quebec and British Columbia's Nisga'a treaty settlement—which by summer 1999 had yet to be ratified by the federal government—Canada has no legislated basis for comanagement south of 60 degrees north latitude. Following the Nisga'a agreement, several media pundits argued that the agreement would become a template for other agreements reached through the B.C. Treaty Commission process. Many Native bands—including some of the Nisga'a—were concerned that too many aboriginal rights had been sacrificed in the deal. That same cloud of doubt surrounded the Treaty Commission process itself; some First Nations would rather enter comanagement negotiations with industry, independent of a treaty, than agree to a land claim negotiation that demands too much compromise. They see treaties and comanagement as mutually exclusive.

---

*The Gitxsan and Wet'suwet'en land claims
began 130 years ago.*

One of the most important legal decisions affecting aboriginal rights in recent years was *Delgamuukw v. British Columbia*. In December 1997, the Supreme Court of Canada overturned a British Columbia court ruling that dismissed claims from the Gitxsan and Wet'suwet'en First Nations to ownership of 58,000 square kilometers (22,400 square miles) of land near the Bulkley, Skeena, and Baine Rivers. The ruling—which allows First Nations a constitutional right to own their ancestral lands and to use them almost entirely as they wish—could lead to treaty settlements involving more than 5 percent (47,390 square kilometers, or 18,300 square miles) of the province's land mass.

The Gitxsan and Wet'suwet'en land claims began 130 years ago. The people pursued their treaty rights based on a 1763 proclamation by George III that recognized North America's aboriginal people as "nations or tribes" of the British Empire and guaranteed them British sovereignty and protection. Essentially, the Supreme Court in 1997 agreed with this claim and ruled that "aboriginal title" to land was never extinguished.

The Supreme Court of Canada ordered a new trial for the claim, ruling that the B.C. trial judge had erred by not taking into account the oral histories presented to establish occupation and use of the lands. The Gitxsan people had spent years interviewing elders, mapping their territory, and fully documenting their traditional use, spending millions of dollars on legal fees in the process. The Supreme Court of Canada judge ruled that the acceptance of oral history could have helped the Gitxsan prove their eligibility for a successful land claim. According to this history, the people had lived on the land before its occupation by the Crown, they had continued to occupy the land, and they were the exclusive occupants at the time of Crown sovereignty.

Delgamuukw has ramifications for all indigenous groups that have not entered into a treaty with the federal government. Among other things, the ruling extended broad-reaching support for the rights of all Native peoples—not just elected tribal councils. It entrenched the notion of respect for Native people's rights and use of the land and said that there ought to be consultation with First Nations people. Although it didn't state that B.C. indigenous groups still own their ancestral lands, it did define land rights as more far-reaching than previously recognized. At the same time, it granted indigenous groups much broader influence than before. Many believe the ruling may give aboriginal communities a form of veto power over industrial development.

Delgamuukw has already been cited in court cases where oil exploration, logging, mining, and other forms of development affect Native people's lives. Litigation may be the only recourse in a province such as British Columbia, whose forests account for nearly half of all the wood logged in Canada. During the 1990s, timber companies logged from 160,000 to 200,000 hectares

(400,000 to 500,000 acres) of B.C. forest every year, 92 percent of that area by clear-cutting.

In November 1998, provincial courts in New Brunswick and British Columbia ruled that indigenous people have a legal right to trees and forests on Crown land. These decisions were complete reversals of previous policy that declared provincial governments to be the sole owners of the forest (with the right to grant exclusive logging licenses). According to the National Aboriginal Forestry Association, the rulings should open the way for more aboriginal groups to file claims asserting their aboriginal right to a share of forest wealth.

CROSSING THE NORTH-SOUTH DIVIDE

For land use management, the 60th parallel that divides Canada's Arctic, North, and boreal forest region from the country's more temperate mid-north is a psychological and intellectual dividing line no less significant than the political dividing line of the 49th parallel that separates Canada from the United States. North of 60, the culture of comanagement is well established. Aboriginal groups such as the Gwich'in, the Sahtu, the Inuvialiut, and the Nunavut are either completing or have already completed comprehensive land claim negotiations. Issues such as cash settlements, land ownership, and the right to comanage are well understood by government and industry. Traditional wisdom of First Nations people is considered crucial to the mix. South of 60, few land claim agreements are in effect. Provincial governments are just beginning to learn the potential of comanagement. And although aboriginal wisdom is now accepted, its application to land use solutions is considered a recent innovation.

For most of the 20th century, the scientific community dismissed traditional knowledge as anecdotal—implying that aboriginal wisdom in forest ecology was less valid than scientific inquiry. Academic and industry racism ("What could aboriginal people possibly know?") has a lot to do with this dismissal. In the

Northwest Territories community of Old Crow, for example, scientists didn't believe Native elders' accounts of giant beavers until archeologists discovered the fossils to prove it. Similarly, a scientific team working on the Al-Pac pulp mill in Alberta denied the existence of barren land caribou in the area until the Arctic Institute—using wisdom obtained from elders in Fort Mackay—established that there had been a southern migration of barren land caribou during the late 1940s because the animals had run out of food.

In discussions of comanagement, skepticism turns into real resistance. When some provincial bureaucrats arrive at their first meeting with an aboriginal group and the subject of comanagement comes up, the first thing they want to do is change the language. "Quite often it's 'cooperative management' rather than comanagement," says Mike Robinson. "They want to introduce euphemisms and rewordings to make the issue more of listening to people in the bush rather than sharing with and stewarding people in the bush. They want to move the discourse from sharing to maintaining ownership—but through consultation. They're not going to give up control because inherent in giving up control is the whole issue of royalties and stumpage, questioning the philosophical underpinnings of science, and giving people who don't subscribe to progress a say in stewarding resources which progress requires."

Comanagement is loaded with legal, fiduciary, and monetary implications. The resistance of some government bureaucrats to its practice is similar to that faced by gay and lesbian groups who have fought to have the term "spouse" apply to a same-sex partner. There are consequences for everyone: from the dollars-and-cents realities of tax restructuring to the more complex social implications of redefining a minority's relationship to the larger community.

The bottom line for industry and government is that comanagement represents a reallocation of power and money that gives

Native people more control over their own land than they have had since the arrival of the Europeans. Under these new agreements, aboriginal communities have the right to control resources, stumpage, royalties paid by developing agents, and so on. More important, comanagement is a deliberate attempt to redefine the central role of science as the determining factor in establishing the overall practice of land use management. It questions some of the basic philosophical assumptions that have governed science for centuries, dating back to Descartes: the idea that science is value-free, its exclusive reliance on deductive or empirical analysis, and its failure to acknowledge the value of traditional wisdom. In this respect, comanagement has been a progressive development.

But comanagement should by no means be considered the only solution to sustainable land use management in the boreal forest. Nor should it be considered a replacement for treaty negotiations. The agreements reached with aboriginal groups in Yukon and the Northwest Territories occurred in a climate of true cooperation, where treaty rights were already entrenched and there was a much larger Native presence in government. South of this region, in what Mike Robinson calls the "provincial mid-north," the same cannot be said.

The success of any comanagement agreement depends, of course, on whose interests are represented at the negotiating table. Does the comanagement agreement truly involve balanced, sustainable use of the land's resources? Are all groups represented, or just the one or two with the most influence? Some critics of comanagement fear that agreements between a company and a powerful group in the community may lead to conflict when many resources or sacred grounds are at stake. Under these circumstances, the only winner is the company, because the comanagement agreement absolves it of sole responsibility for how the resources are used.

Similarly, federal and provincial governments look good when a comanagement agreement is signed. Such agreements not only make good press; they often remove the political headache of having to deal with a land claim negotiation or—where a treaty already exists—of having to face litigation by a Native group seeking the ability, through the court system, to exercise its treaty rights. Some aboriginal groups—exhausted by the glacial progress of land claim negotiations with government—see comanagement with companies as a fall-back position, the quickest and easiest way to regain some control of their resources. But that approach may be unnecessary.

"If First Nations are interested in managing their resources," wonders Don Sullivan of Manitoba's Future Forest Alliance, "why do they need to comanage it with multinationals? First Nations have an unprecedented amount of rights that are continually being reaffirmed by the courts to such a point that if they really wanted to exercise those rights, they would essentially have control of those resources within an area defined by [*Delgamuukw*] as a traditional land use area."

Regardless of the courts, however, it appears that some level of comanagement will be inevitable in boreal forest communities as resource companies become more progressive and aboriginal groups more active in controlling their traditional lands. James Allen, a member of the Champagne-Aishihik band—a community of some 850 people about 160 kilometers (100 miles) northwest of Whitehorse in Yukon—acknowledges that comanagement of development projects may be easier to attain in northern communities such as his own, where treaties already exist. The Development Assessment Process is guaranteed by his band's land claims agreement, and traditional knowledge is a big part of the process. But Allen, who runs a contracting business that conducts traditional knowledge research, oral history projects, and culture camps for a variety of clients ranging from Japanese students to the Yukon government, believes that First Nations people in other boreal regions may not have the luxury of waiting for treaties to be signed before considering comanagement. "If we're going to live in today's society," he says, "we have to let some development happen too, because it creates work for us. I mean, we don't all live off trapping anymore." At the same time, he adds, development that is informed by traditional knowledge is less likely to take the land's resources for granted. Whether it's a heritage site or sacred ground that needs to be preserved, or new wildlife regulations that could be written with First Nations' input, says Allen, "you have to steer development around those kinds of issues."

If more communities in the boreal region adopted this approach to development, who knows how much more forest could be preserved?

CHAPTER 11

Return of the Halo: Reforesting *Borealis*

We do not sustain the forest; the forest sustains us.
—Herb Hammond, *The Boreal Forest:*
Options for Ecologically Responsible Use

In dealing with the many issues related to the boreal forest, a number of urgent questions come to mind: How will the world's northern countries be able to preserve their boreal ecosystems in the face of climate change and the current rate of industrial development? Can alternative forestry be promoted, on a local level, that might prolong, or even restore, the boreal forest in regions where it is imperiled? And finally, who among us will have the vision and the will to promote this better way for the forest?

Part of the answer to this last question occurred to me in October 1998, as I sat in a cafeteria in Varska, Estonia, about 8 kilometers (5 miles) west of the Russian border. I was listening to a speech by Arne Naess, the venerable Norwegian philosopher, father of deep ecology, and author of such books as *Ecology, Community and Lifestyle.* Naess had just finished defining his use of the term "spontaneous experience" (a willful act of concentration that allows one to recognize hundreds of things in a single moment, such as the simple gesture of gazing at a flower) when he paused to recall a protest he had attended some years earlier.

In the middle of winter, when the temperature was -70°F, more than a thousand people had gathered to demand that a hydroelectric dam, scheduled for construction near a traditional Sámi homeland in the north of Norway, be scrapped.

Naess recalled that six hundred police officers arrived at the scene—nearly one cop for every two protesters. As the police approached, the demonstrators lay down on the road, remaining still. "They began to drag us away," said Naess. "And I said to one of them, 'May I stay a while longer? I am studying police behavior.' Because I was polite, they let me stay. So when they came back later, one of them *asked* if he could take me away. I said, 'Just a minute,' then lay down to be dragged away."

ECOFORESTRY: RESPECTING THE ECOSYSTEM

American ecologist Bill Devall, writing an essay on eco-activism in the forest, recalled a story about Mahatma Gandhi. In the 1940s, a group of journalists went to visit the great spiritual leader at his ashram in India. Asked what motivated his passionate service to the poor, Gandhi replied, "I serve no one but myself." It was an ironic statement, to be sure. Gandhi was not telling reporters that he was selfish but that serving the poor was an act of supreme fulfillment that nourished his inner self. Like Gandhi, whose inner self was "broad and deep," Devall argues that people who are committed to preserving the forest and other ecosystems "serve themselves" by taking responsibility for the world around them. Whereas Gandhi did it by helping the downtrodden, conservationists do it by acting on behalf of the "salmon, salamanders, fungi, fallen trees, rivers, streams, bears, mountain lions and the great ecological processes—fire, wind, rain and decay—that sustain the life of the forest/watershed/mountains."

By this definition, people like Arne Naess—not to mention the thousand or so protesters who joined him in the subzero freeze of northern winter to protest a hydroelectric dam development— were also serving their inner selves. In doing so, they subscribed to what Herb Hammond has referred to as ecology's hierarchy of systems. Natural resources, including land and water, are superior to cultures because cultures couldn't exist without these resources. Cultures, in turn, are superior to the economy because the economy couldn't exist without culture. Therefore, the economy should serve the people, who, in turn, should serve the forest—not the reverse.

Hammond is a forestry consultant from the Kootenay region of southeastern British Columbia. During the 1970s, while working for timber giants such as Weyerhaeuser and Crown Zellerbach, he began to realize that the scientific model alone could not sustain forest ecosystems or the people and animal species that depend on them. So he left the forest industry to do applied research in soil and water degradation and practical planning systems, to teach silviculture and forest ecology, and to act as a consultant to First Nations groups, environmental NGOs, and community organizations. Working with First Nation groups such as the Nisga'a Tribal Council, the Gitxsan-Wet'suwet'en Hereditary Chiefs, and the Kluskus Band, Hammond learned, as he put it, "to connect my heart to my brain."

How can control of the forests shift from governments and transnational corporations back to the community?

Throughout his two decades of working as a forest consultant, the same vision kept appearing to Hammond: a vision of smaller-scale, community-based forestry that serves local needs without depleting the forest. The question was how to bring about this kind of change in communities whose very existence depends on supplying the global forest industry with raw material. How can control of the forests shift from governments and transnational corporations back to the community? In the face of globalization, how can society move toward sustainable forest use without a corresponding rise in unemployment?

In 1991, Hammond wrote *Seeing the Forest Among the Trees: The Case for Wholistic Forest Use,* a visionary guide to responsible forestry that offered workable alternatives for sustainable land use management that foresters and conservationists alike could embrace. The book proposed a new model of forestry that would sustain not only the environment but also the economy and communities within it. The model is based on two principles:

- *Ecological responsibility.* Human use must protect and maintain the integrity of the whole forest.
- *Balanced use.* All forest users, human and nonhuman, are guaranteed a fair and protected land base.

These principles form the foundation of ecocentric forestry, or ecoforestry, a philosophy defined in a recent book of the same title as a dedication "to maintain and restore full functioning, natural forest ecosystems in perpetuity, while harvesting forest goods on a sustainable basis." The word "sustainable" means that logging is conducted in a manner that respects the integrity of the ecosystem and allows all its life-forms to regenerate. Proponents of this approach believe that a forest is much greater than the sum of its trees. It is, as media critic Jerry Mander once claimed, "a community of hundreds of thousands of life forms that collaborate for sustainability." An experienced professional who embraces this view is known as an ecoforester. Of those ecoforesters proposing changes in the boreal region, Herb Hammond is among the most prominent.

As Hammond pointed out in *Seeing the Forest Among the Trees,* the old forestry model of assigning five- to twenty-year logging licenses often ruins the forest and leaves nothing for future generations. Hammond would like to replace these licenses with forest use agreements that call for 250- to 500-year plans. Shorter licenses tend to put pressure on companies to achieve the largest yield possible to maximize profits. Under the longer cycle, the natural disturbance cycle could provide a more sustainable blue-print for logging. Companies under such long-term license arrangements could organize timber-cutting areas that encom-pass the range of patterns created by fire, wind, and decay.

For more remote forest areas with little or no human presence, Hammond recommends a combination of full protected status and protected reserves or "landscape networks" (nonindustrial forest zones that are connected by various "holes" where some small-scale activities take place). Generally speaking, Hammond recommends five categories of forest use in the boreal region:

- *Culture Zones.* Areas defined by First Nations as required for the protection and maintenance of their culture.
- *Ecotourism and Public Recreation Zones.* Areas set aside to maintain a diversity of forest-based recreation and tourism.
- *Wildlife Zones.* Special habitat for various animal species that have not been protected in either large protected reserves or protected landscape networks.
- *Trapping Zones.* Selected riparian zones set aside for small-scale activities such as hunting and trapping. (These activi-ties must be widely dispersed throughout the landscape, and trappers are required to protect ecosystem composition and structures.)
- *Timber Management Zones.* Identified by timber interests as stable forest ecosystem types capable of supporting continu-ous reforestation in reasonable periods of time.

Such forest use zones would not be ecologically or socially desirable in every boreal context. The balance of the various zones in a given area would depend on the ecological makeup and the desires of the human population of the area. As Hammond points out, some regions would not be appropriate for any form of timber extraction other than small-scale, partial cutting to satisfy local needs.

Hammond's ecologically based model of forest use also specifies what type of logging would be allowed in a timber extraction zone. Clear-cutting would not be allowed, as it has been shown to intensify global climate change by creating drier atmospheric conditions and destroying the process by which soil generates its nutrients. Clear-cut logging sites are usually 40 hectares (100 acres) or larger, with sharp boundaries designed for logging efficiency rather than for maintenance of the ecosystem. As Hammond notes, clear-cuts do substantially more damage to the ecosystem than fires:

- Clear-cuts remove all trees of all sizes, while fires leave behind trunks, snags, and sometimes single trees or groups of living trees.
- Boreal clear-cuts take out some of the oldest trees in the forest—even reaching the moist lowland areas along creeks, streams, and rivers that fires don't get to.
- Unlike fires, clear-cuts "homogenize the landscape," creating identical patches of seedling-to-middle-aged stands of boreal trees.
- Wildfires are followed by a succession of herbs and shrubs that provide browsing for moose and snowshoe hares, at the same time opening up the forest soils to receive nutrients. Clear-cuts are followed by brush clearing and pesticide use, which shortens the herb/shrub phase.

Hammond does not recommend single-tree removal, currently in vogue for temperate forests, either—the process is too slow, costly, and impractical. Instead—as mentioned—he suggests that communities take the lead from the taiga's unique cycles of natural disturbance such as fire, decay, and wind (the "blowback" of fallen trees). With this approach, some portions of cut forest could even be larger than in temperate forests because the cutting would encompass the range of patterns created by these disturbances. Logging would also occur at intervals equal to "the longest timeframe between successive natural disturbances in a particular area." This practice would allow enough time for each area to recover through reforestation.

Another obsolete method in the boreal forest is full-tree logging, the conventional practice of removing trees from the landscape with the branches and needles intact. Full-tree logging lowers the percentage of nutrients available for the next stand of trees. Stem-only logging, Hammond's alternative, removes branches and needles at the site, leaving them in the forest to decompose and thus provide enough nitrogen to support subsequent tree growth.

An ecosystem-based planning model in the boreal forest would also prohibit the use of pesticides and slash-burning in timber management zones, exclude logging from poorly drained sites or those with high water tables, limit the combined area of roadways and landings to no more than 10 percent of the total cutting area (logging routes would have to be determined before cutting), and allow logging on frozen ground only when soil moisture is high enough to prevent long-term soil degradation.

Although this plan seems ambitious, Hammond is no utopian. He doesn't believe, for example, that this model could be applied immediately on a large scale. Throughout his consulting work and in his published articles, he emphasizes that such broad standards for ecologically responsible timber management should first be applied on a trial basis in various boreal regions—preferably in smaller forest communities where comanagement agreements can be reached. Only after a long monitoring and evaluation period—one hundred years at the very least—should the model be adopted for larger areas. In the meantime, though, Hammond wants to see an end to large-scale commercial timber cutting "until we have a much better understanding of the functioning of this fragile and critical ecosystem ... Only through this process of careful scrutiny will we be able to come to grips with the biological limits of the boreal forest."

REFORESTING SCOTLAND: A BOREAL SUCCESS STORY

The people of Scotland know those limits all too well. Once upon a time, the forests of Scotland were part of the boreal forest's green halo. Less than three hundred years ago, the great Caledonian Forest—from Caledonia, a name the Romans gave to Scotland, meaning "wooded heights"—was a landscape rich with native Scots pine, birch, rowan, and aspen, and boreal flora such as the twinflower. Wildlife species such as the beaver, wild boar, lynx, moose, brown bear, and wolf roamed the woods. Birds such as the capercaillie, crested tit, and Scottish crossbill were common. The Caledonian Forest composed the westernmost corner of the European boreal forest, covering an area of more than 1.5 million hectares (3.7 million acres) in the northern Highlands and one-quarter of Scotland's land base. Today, only 1 percent of the original Scottish forest remains standing.

Although deforestation has a long history in Scotland (tree cutting for agriculture goes back as far as the Neolithic age), the disappearance of Scotland's forest really began in the wake of the failed Highland uprisings in the 18th century. The English government, hoping to prevent another Jacobite rebellion, decided to construct miles of military roads. These roads ripped through the Caledonian Forest, opening up the Highlands to the government army. To reduce the risk of reprisal attacks or ambush from the Scots, the English cut even larger tracts of forest, turning some of the leftover timber into sailing masts for the navy.

Following the uprisings, Highland chiefs who once stood against the English were charged heavy taxes and were forced to sell even larger tracts of forest than what they had already lost. In the forest clearing that followed, villagers tried to grow crops.

But the Highland's harsh and unpredictable weather made agriculture difficult, and few farmers were successful. The Highland forests soon became a "wet desert"—an impoverished and barren landscape that could not produce enough resources for its own people. Burdened by the high cost of rent, villagers were on the brink of starvation and were soon forced to leave the forest, abandoning the countryside and moving south to the rapidly growing cities of Glasgow, Edinburgh, Dundee, and Aberdeen. Those who could afford the journey left Scotland to seek a new way of life in Canada and the United States. This mass exodus broke the link to generations of ancestors, and a unique culture of crafts, music, and language vanished from the Highland landscape.

Today, only 1 percent of the
original Scottish forest remains standing.

The forest also disappeared. Virtually every large mammal species, except for the deer, was either forced out of the woods by logging or hunted to extinction. The last known wolf in Scotland was shot in 1743. By the 1820s, the capercaillie and other rare birds of the region had almost disappeared.

Today, the total forest cover in Scotland has risen to 14 percent, but most of that forest has been created as monoculture tree farms. Less than 1 percent of Scotland's original forests remain. The native pine woods have been reduced to thirty-five isolated remnants—small pieces of forest now threatened by an exploding deer population. With no natural predator other than humans, the deer have multiplied at an unsustainable rate and are laying waste to seedlings and younger trees. At the same time, an increase in sheep farming is destroying even more of the forest, as the sheep graze on younger trees.

Because the land is not protected from overgrazing, and there are no emerging trees to replace the old ones, many believe that the last remnants of old-growth could disappear completely in the next century. Another problem can be found in the replanted forests where the only species is Sitka spruce. According to one observer, some of the worst silviculture in Scotland can be found "on exposed sites in the uplands where Sitka spruce plantations have seen no management since they were planted, and where no thinning takes place."

Land ownership poses yet another obstacle to reforestation. Scotland is one of the few places in the world where anyone can buy large areas of public property. Thus, many of the surviving forest areas in Scotland are private land. Some owners are absentee landlords who are not necessarily concerned about how their use of the land affects surrounding ecosystems. Others encourage a rise in the deer population to attract tourist revenue for sports hunting.

Thankfully, it appears that a concerted effort is finally being made to save the Scottish boreal forest. The last three decades have given birth to a number of grassroots organizations working on ecological restoration—a recent field of science dedicated to restoring the earth's ecological balance. Many of these organizations rely on volunteers—people willing to spend weekends or days off planting hundreds of thousands of trees and then building fences to protect the younger trees from deer and sheep populations. After the fences are built, seeds are planted to produce young saplings; the fences are then removed once the trees are established.

Groups such as Trees for Life are leading the way. In the northwestern Highlands region of Glen Affric, Trees for Life covered the cost of fencing 190 hectares (470 acres) of land dedicated to forest regeneration and expansion. In total, more than 108,000 Scots pine seedlings and other native trees have been protected by fences funded by this group. By 1998, Trees for Life staff and volunteers had planted more than 230,000 Scots pines and broad-leaved trees.

Another encouraging development has been the return of the Scottish diaspora. According to David Whyte of Reforesting Scotland, families that long ago abandoned the Highland forests of their ancestors for better lives in Canada and the United States are returning to settle down, bringing with them the culture and skills passed down through generations. Reflecting the rise in national pride that has accompanied the renewed independence movement, these people are creating their own forests or small woodlands and thus are playing a key role in regenerating the Scottish boreal forest. "This is where [they] can act as advisors in pointing the community in the right direction," says Whyte. "The result has given the people a sense of ownership and a clear understanding of how they can achieve sustainable and economic benefits for future generations. Without this kind of enthusiasm from people of all ages, it's clear that the forest would not make any progress at all. At last, we are beginning to get somewhere."

THE FOREST AS VILLAGE

The promotion of community-based forestry is steeped in pragmatism. Because communities in or near the forest have a long-term commitment to remaining in the same area, they are more likely to ensure the long-term survival of the forest than a transnational timber company whose head office is thousands of miles away. All it takes is a downturn in the economy or an effective campaign blitz by a group such as Greenpeace, and the average transnational corporation will pack its bags faster than you can say "clear-cut." This fact perhaps provides the best explanation for the effectiveness of local strategies in changing boreal forest land use practices.

In northern Sweden, conservation groups are experimenting with the forest village concept to preserve old-growth forests in their country. Urpo Taskinen, a member of the Swedish Society for Nature Conservation, lives in a village of about 250 people surrounded by 10,000 hectares (25,000 acres) of old-growth forest. Just before the 4th Taiga Rescue Network conference, Taskinen was approached by nine people—most of them senior citizens—who wanted to form a conservation study group.

> *Because communities in or near the forest have a*
> *long-term commitment to remaining in the same area,*
> *they are more likely to ensure the long-term survival of the*
> *forest than a transnational timber company whose*
> *head office is thousands of miles away.*

Taskinen introduced the group to the Step Ahead program, an organizing kit that uses information about endangered species to establish how valuable a forest is and whether it should be protected. Taskinen's study group eventually produced a report recommending more than a hundred forests in the region for protection. Step Ahead methodology has been adopted by all the forest companies of Sweden and is now being applied in Norway, Finland, and Russia. Its main appeal, says Taskinen, is that you don't need a Ph.D. in forest ecology to understand it. "One of the things with Step Ahead is that you don't need to be an expert—it's better if you're not. This is really a local solution: it's simple, it's effective, and now we see the results ... Many of the people in the village want to preserve these forests, they want to use them for hunting, fishing, and tourism. And these people are not experts. They have learned this method." Although Step Ahead may not, in itself, lead to legislation for protected areas in Sweden, forest companies are at least beginning to take notice.

At the 4th Taiga Rescue Network conference in Estonia, there was no shortage of people willing to take heroic measures to promote the forest village concept. One man from Finland, Herald

Helander, told me that in 1986 he decided to dedicate his life to forest conservation when he learned that timber companies were targeting the last remaining old-growth forests in his native Lapland. Helander, who was working as a site manager on a building project in Indonesia at the time, immediately got on a plane, moved to the Lapland forest with his wife, Margarete, and built a log cabin. At fifty-three, he decided to become a forest activist. "I totally changed my lifestyle," he told me outside a seminar room at the University of Tartu. "I decided to give up my job and totally engage in trying to save our last remnants of wilderness forests."

Before long, he was writing newspaper articles about the Finnish forest industry's assault on the boreal forest. Finnish newspaper editors were not eager to publish the articles, however, so Helander decided to peddle them in Germany. After all, Germany was a major consumer of boreal wood products from Finland, so readers might be interested in learning about the forestry practices of one of Scandinavia's Big Three producer countries.

According to Helander, the articles caused enough of a stir back home to help curb some of the more destructive clear-cutting practices in Finland. With this success behind him, he approached the German papers with an article advocating a modern version of the medieval forest village as a cure for unemployment in Lapland. Although the region once had a thriving local culture, Finnish Lapland had disintegrated in recent years into a wasteland of alcoholism, domestic violence, and broken homes, thanks to an unemployment rate that never fell below 30 percent. For many young people, the only hope of survival was to move south.

Helander's concept of forest villages involved resettling people from economically depressed areas into small pockets of second-growth forest. The idea was to build smaller, self-sufficient communities that relied on the land's resources for livelihood but maintained the ecological structure of the forest. Based on the bush economy, the forest village would require assistance from the logging industry. Instead of logging the forest and sending raw logs to faraway pulp mills, timber companies would create local jobs in wood processing. Using second-growth timber directly from the region, local residents would create value-added wood products such as furniture and building materials, thus earning an income without sacrificing the area's valuable old-growth pine forests, which contained trees as old as five hundred years.

As luck would have it, Helander's feature on forest villages appeared in the German press the same week that Finland's president was in Germany on a state visit. The coverage generated so much interest back home that Helander was soon getting calls from university professors eager to explore the potential of forest villages. Since then, he's worked with scientists, indigenous people, and NGOs to introduce the model in selected communities. "We're still in discussion with forest managers—we speak with each other," said Helander, adding that change does not take place overnight. "Before, as an activist, I was stopping [logging] machines. I was sitting in court, I was fined. There was no possibility [of dialogue]. They just did what they wanted. But now times have changed."

Helander and his wife still live in that log cabin in the tiny village of Ivalo. Using solar paneling for heat and a small wind generator for electricity, they have no television set, telephone, fax, or computer. But they don't feel cut off from the outside world. "I work with personal contact and I work with the press," says Helander. "The people come to me."

Consumer Countries: Making Better Choices

It's not only the people living in boreal countries who need to change their habits to save the taiga. Consumer countries—including both governments and corporations that buy old-growth timber products from the boreal belt—need to reexamine their shopping habits. In Germany, NGO groups such as Urgewald raise public awareness about their country's role as an international consumer of boreal forest wood products. "If we get information from a local community that there is German [investment], either through a German company, German bilateral aid or German multilateral aid via the World Bank, or through German people consuming products that are made from that area, then we start reacting to that," Urgewald's Jutta Kill explains.

One German politician, returning home from a recent tour of Canadian forests—the source of many of Germany's wood products—wrote a scathing parliamentary report that sparked a nationwide debate on the indigenous rights of Canadian aboriginals. News about the struggle of the Lubicon and other aboriginal groups fighting to preserve their traditional way of life in the face of giant projects can have a big impact overseas. Many European companies have stopped buying wood products from countries where human rights abuses or unresolved land claims are an issue. "People in Europe, in general, are so far removed from natural forests and different ways of life that by exposing them to people who still live that way, you really get an amazing change in their perception," said Kill.

In Japan—where the average house lasts no more than twenty-five years before it's torn down—the Ishida Architects Association is collaborating with Friends of the Earth to promote the idea of eco-housing. The purpose of the project is to reduce Japanese consumption of Siberian wood products while raising awareness about wasteful housing construction practices, reforming Japanese building codes, and offering alternative energy ideas and more efficient, less wasteful house-building methods. The ideal home is produced from domestic, non-old-growth timber, is run primarily by solar power, and is built to last for at least a hundred years.

The model structure, known as the OM Solar House, is located in Tokyo. Opened in June 1999, the house is being used for press conferences and meetings with Japanese government officials, construction and trading companies, and progressive architects.

One of the key focus groups is Japanese home magazines, which influence consumer demand for certain housing construction styles. "To show the effects of consumption on overseas forests, then point to an eco-house as a positive example of where we need to go—we're excited about that possibility," says Josh Newell of Friends of the Earth–Japan.

Toward the Future: A Sense of Urgency

Over the next hundred years, the human community faces a challenge far more daunting than any that has come before: How are we going to preserve our limited natural resources on a planet whose population of 5 billion is expected to double in the first quarter of the 21st century? What will be left of our forests in a hundred years if we continue to strip-mine them according to the dictates of supply-and-demand economics? What difference will mass reforestation make if we don't significantly reduce our consumption of fossil fuels?

The biggest challenge may be overcoming our collective pessimism. Poll after poll suggests that people *do* care about what's happening to the planet and want to do something about it. According to a 1998 survey conducted by the World Wildlife Fund, an overwhelming majority of Americans—89 percent—are concerned about environmental issues. But only one in four believe that effective action will be taken to ensure a healthy environment for future generations.

Such pessimism cannot be easily dismissed. The pressures of a global economy—expressed through shareholders and bankers—force most businesses into an inordinate focus on short-term financial results. Why should they care about the long-term consequences of their activities when they're trying to erase next year's looming deficit?

But some corporations are beginning to realize that "eco-friendly" business is good for the bottom line. Over the last decade, IBM has reduced its carbon dioxide emissions by 6 million tonnes, saving the company U.S.$525 million in the process. British Petroleum made corporate and environmental history by lending its support to the Kyoto Agreement on climate change. And Noranda Inc. has recognized the need "to make the principles of sustainable development a fundamental part of our business strategies and day-to-day operations."

Recent studies of soil erosion, increased nitrogen and sulfate emissions, projected climate change, and patterns of natural disturbance suggest that the forest industry needs to reexamine its assumptions about "sustainable yield" in the boreal forest. Many scientists argue that forest companies should be forced to absorb the costs of resource use, including lost recreation potential, degraded fisheries, the need for fire control, and road construction. At the same time, forest owners and timber companies need to recognize the many benefits that growing forests provide—even to the point of being taxed for the amount of forest cut. Some conservationists argue that governments should impose a carbon tax on resource companies whose destruction of the forest contributes to the release of carbon into the atmosphere. "If carbon taxes are assessed in proportion to net carbon emission of each country," write F. Stuart Chapin and Gail Whiteman, "there will suddenly be a large economic benefit to growing forests, even if these forests are converted into products that decompose more slowly than they would in the forest."

At the same time, governments must reexamine the host of incentives they offer to the logging, petroleum, and mining industries: low timber license fees, multimillion-dollar development grants, and subsidized logging roads, to name a few.

The encouraging news is that boreal forests have become a testing ground for innovative experiments in locally based forest planning—ideas whose application could serve as a model for other forest ecosystems. The promotion of such ecoforestry models as Herb Hammond's should get a big push from global strategies such as the Forest Frontiers Initiative, a five-year multidisciplinary program sponsored by the World Resources Institute and designed to promote stewardship in the world's last remaining frontier forests. The initiative will seek to influence investment, policy, and public opinion in five regions, of which the Russian taiga is the largest. Working with project partners such as the World Conservation Monitoring Center and the World Wildlife Fund, the World Resources Institute is building a network of policy makers, activists, investors, and researchers to assist local organizations in promoting sustainable alternatives to forest destruction that will serve the entire community.

Even technology is playing a role in saving the taiga. The use of satellite mapping to identify and monitor the attrition of old-growth forests has already convinced major timber suppliers like ENSO to avoid logging in these places altogether. Now, even pulp mill operators have an opportunity to demand non-old-growth wood products from their suppliers.

A Return to Innocence

The future, we are always told, is in our youth. Scanning a lecture hall during the 4th Taiga Rescue Network conference, I look for the future face of activism in the boreal forest and find it in the playful exuberance of twenty-year-old Daniel Thorell, a handsome young Swede with a mischievous smile and an easygoing manner. Thorell appeared to enjoy himself throughout the conference—despite some of the longer lectures—and was often seen joking with his pal Marcus or lying in the arms of Pernilla, his shy, twenty-one-year-old girlfriend. All three are members of Faltbiologerna, a conservationist youth organization with chapters in Sweden, Norway, and Denmark.

Chatting in an old firemen's hall in Tartu one night after dinner —as a group of Estonian dancers were doing a traditional waltz on the floor below us—Thorell told me that his group, in the last decade, has raised one million Swedish Crowns to purchase chunks of old-growth forest. Whenever the group finds a forest that needs to be protected, members contact the forest company under license and try to persuade it not to log. "If we don't buy it they might cut it down," he says. "Last year, we bought two forests." They weren't very large—one was only 2 hectares (5 acres), the other 20 (50 acres). But this symbolic action had an immediate effect on the public. What did it say about the government's priorities that in a country as rich as Sweden, forest preservation depended on bake sales and benefit concerts organized by youth?

Thorell and his companions also converted 100,000 Crowns into gold coins, put them in a treasure chest, and presented them to the environment minister. They wanted the government to use the cash to protect the forest. "Youth have new ideas and they're not afraid of doing different things, like adults," Thorell explained. "Young people act the way they feel. They're more spontaneous, and that's one reason I think there's a big difference from an organization that has adult leaders. We don't have leaders tell us what to do."

With such thinking, our halo may return yet.

Epilogue

December 1998

Thirty-seven years after Yuri Gagarin glimpsed the boreal forest from *Vostok,* an unmanned satellite followed the same path in space, recording images of the earth's land surface directly below it. The data, read by scientists back on the planet, showed a marked decline in ancient forests in the Leningrad region that earlier, on-the-ground estimates had failed to detect. That information was passed on to an environmental group, which then passed it on to the Svetogorsk pulp-and-paper company, whose mill on the Finnish-Russian border had been using old-growth timber from Leningrad for years. Faced with dramatic new evidence of a depleted forest ecosystem, company officials did the unthinkable: they announced to the world that they would no longer use old-growth forests to produce Svetogorsk's pulp and paper.

The announcement seemed to herald a new beginning for the boreal forests of Russia. It also set a precedent for sustainable forest use around the green halo; the same satellite information that had been sent to Svetogorsk was now on its way to companies in Sweden, Austria, Germany, the United Kingdom, and the Netherlands. If this data-recording system were to be applied internationally—and the results of each survey released to governments and media simultaneously—there would be no telling how much forest could be saved.

If that were to happen, perhaps a day will come when cosmonauts or astronauts, viewing the world from outer space, can see the boreal forest in all its original splendor. Perhaps instead of chessboard grids and a Swiss cheese landscape, they will gaze in wonder at the endless belt of green that Yuri Gagarin once saw. Perhaps within this giant green halo, there will still be vast chunks of forest where human beings have never set foot. Or where—in the small, ancient places in which forest people did exist—the thundering sound of caribou hooves can still be heard in the distance. Where the solitude of the taiga is broken only by the call of a red wolf on a hillside, and the stillness of a boreal lake shattered only by the ripples of jumping trout. Where it is still possible to gaze, like Yuri from *Doctor Zhivago*, over an endless pine forest and be humbled by the majesty of its scale and the power of its silence.

Notes

CHAPTER I

PAGE 4   Definitions of taiga, William O. Pruitt, *Boreal Ecology* (London: Edward Arnold, 1978), pp. 3–4.

PAGE 5   Forest's importance to Karelian economy, Renfrey Clarke, "Environmentalists in Russia Fight Old Growth Logging," posted on the *Green Left Weekly* website. Available at <www.greenleft.org.au/>.

PAGE 5   Percentages of productive forest land, background paper to the 4th Taiga Rescue Network conference, Tartu, Estonia, October 6–10, 1998, p. 10.

PAGE 5   "Largest remaining functioning boreal forest," Greenpeace press release, January 10, 1997.

PAGES 7–8   Tamarack and black spruce from the Boreal Forest map, published by *Canadian Geographic* and Environment Canada.

PAGE 9   Peat moss spread, M.J. Apps et al., "The Changing Role of Circumpolar Boreal Forests and Tundra in the Global Carbon Cycle," *Water, Air, and Soil Pollution* (1993).

PAGE 11   For information on lichens, I'm indebted to a variety of sources, most notably the North American Lichen Project website constructed by American lichenologists Stephen and Sylvia Sharnoff, coauthors with the Canadian Museum of Nature's Irwin M. Brodo of *Lichens of North America*, forthcoming from Yale University Press.

PAGE 11   Uses of Labrador tea, *Traditional Ways of Healing from Addictions*, prepared by Hollow Water First Nation, Native Alcohol and Drug Addiction Program, p. 10, (1998).

PAGE 15   "The sheer distances," Pruitt, *Boreal Ecology,* p. 66.

PAGE 15   "The Throng," quoted in *Boreal Ecology,* pp. 66–67.

PAGE 16   "Forest, forest, FOREST," Arne Naess, "The Heart of the Forest," in *Ecoforestry: The Art and Science of Sustainable Forest Use,* eds. Alan R. Drengson and Duncan M. Taylor (Gabriola Island, BC: New Society, 1997), p. 259.

CHAPTER 2

PAGE 21   All quotes from Garry and Raymond Raven are from interviews with the author.

PAGE 24   "Preference for country foods," Hugh Brody, *Maps and Dreams* (Vancouver: Douglas & McIntyre, 1981), pp. 209–210.

PAGE 25   Inga-Maria Mulk, *Sámi Cultural Heritage,* Ajtte Swedish Mountain and Sámi Museum, Jokkmokk, Sweden, (1997).

PAGE 25   "The decision on where to harvest," F. Stuart Chapin and Gail Whiteman, "Sustainable Development of the Boreal Forest: Interaction of Ecological, Social and Business Feedbacks," Ecological Society of America, 1998.

PAGE 26   "If you dam," from a lecture by Arne Naess at the Varska Sanitorium, Estonia, October 8, 1998.

PAGE 26   Meaning of "Lapp," *An Introduction to the Sámi People.* Available at <www.itv.se/boreale/samigeng1.htm>.

PAGE 27   "In people's memories," Mulk, *Sámi Cultural Heritage.*

PAGE 27   "Mental maps," ibid.

PAGE 29   Hendrik Relve, a member of the Estonian Green movement, delivered these remarks in a presentation at the 4th Taiga Rescue Network conference, Tartu, Estonia, October 6–10, 1998.

PAGE 30   All quotes from Natalia Cherbakova and Olga Galchinova are from interview with the author. I'm grateful to Mary Rees and Stephanie Hitztaler, who provided translation.

CHAPTER 3

PAGE 36   Yukon forest burned, Jamie Bastedo, *Reaching North: Celebrating the Subarctic* (Red Deer, AB: Red Deer College Press, 1998), p. 174.

PAGE 37   Fire's effect on tree species from the Quebec Forest Industries Association website. Available at <www.aifq.qc.ca/>.

PAGE 38   Clear-cuts compared with fire, Elizabeth May, *At the Cutting Edge: The Crisis in Canada's Forests* (Toronto: Key Porter, 1998), pp. 15–17. See also Herb Hammond, *Seeing the Forest Among the Trees* (Vancouver: Polestar, 1991).

PAGE 39   People's use of fire, Bastedo, *Reaching North*, pp. 175–76.

PAGES 39–40   Travelers' brushfires, ibid, p. 180.

PAGE 40   Larger fires, The Boreal Forest map, published by *Canadian Geographic* and Environment Canada.

PAGES 41–42   *Western Canada Wilderness Committee Report*, 17(3) (1998).

PAGES 42–43   Fire fighting, UN Office for the Coordination of Humanitarian Affairs, *Russian Federation–Environmental Emergency/Forest Fires OCHA Situation Report No. 3,* October 13, 1998.

PAGE 43   Effects of exposure to smoke, "Fires on Khabarovsk, Russian Far East," press release by the L'auravetl'an Information Center of the Indigenous Peoples of Russia, October 30, 1998.

PAGE 43   Smoke inhalation, Nonna Chernyakova and Russell Working, "Hundreds Battle Raging Khabarovsk Fires," *Vladivostok News* website. Available at <vlad.tribnet.com/1998/iss162/front.html>.

PAGE 43   "Even if poachers," "Siberian Fires Declared Global Disaster," *Environmental News Network,* October 26, 1998.

CHAPTER 4

PAGE 44   "Global Warming Reaches Far North," *Globe and Mail,* September 14, 1998.

PAGE 47   "Our ability to quantify," J.T. Houghton et al., eds., *Climate Change 1995—The Science of Climate Change* (Cambridge: Cambridge University Press, 1996). This document, Volume I of the report of the Intergovernmental Panel on Climate Change, is quoted in a 1998 report prepared for the David Suzuki Foundation by John Last, Konia Trouton, and David Pengelly, *Taking Our Breath Away: The Health Effects of Air Pollution and Climate Change*, p. 6.

PAGE 48   Extent of logging, John Houghton, *Global Warming: The Complete Briefing* (Cambridge: Cambridge University Press, 1997), p. 189, cited in *Taking Our Breath Away*, p. 30.

PAGE 51   Nansen Environmental and Remote Sensing Center Report, Bergen, Norway, May 1996.

PAGE 51   A.M. Solomon and R. Leemans, "Boreal Forest Carbon Stocks and Wood Supply: Past, Present and Future Responses to Changing Climate, Agriculture and Species Availability," *Journal of Agriculture and Forest Meteorology* 84 (1997).

PAGE 52   "Boreal Mayhem: The Effects of Recent Human Activities on Boreal Landscapes," *Western Canada Wildnerness Committee Report* 17(3) (1998).

PAGES 53–54   *Canada Country Study: Climate Impacts and Adaptation,* vol. III, Environment Canada, 1997.

PAGE 54   "If Climate Changes, Who Is Vulnerable? Panels Offer Projections," *New York Times,* September 30, 1997. The other quote from Glenn Juday is from an interview with the author.

CHAPTER 5

PAGE 58   Anders Ockerman, "Changing Forests, Changing Ideas: A Cultural History and Possible Futures of Forestry," a lecture delivered at the 4th Taiga Rescue Network conference in Estonia, October 6–10, 1998.

PAGE 59   F. Stuart Chapin and Gail Whiteman, "Sustainable Development of the Boreal Forest: Interaction of Ecological, Social and Business Feedbacks," Ecological Society of America, 1998. Published by Conservation Ecology at <www.consecol.org./Journal/vol2/iss2/art12/>.

PAGE 61   John Ralston Saul, *The Doubter's Companion: A Dictionary of Aggressive Common Sense* (Toronto: Penguin, 1995), p. 290.

PAGES 62–63   Taiga Rescue Network, "Underlying Causes of Forest Loss—Joint NGO Statement," December 1998.

PAGE 63–64   Thomas Waggener, Charles Backman, and Ekaterina Gataulina, "Outlook for Russian Forest Product Trade with the People's Republic of China," CINTRAFOR abstract, 1996.

CHAPTER 6

PAGES 66–67   Boris Pasternak, *Doctor Zhivago,* originally published in 1958 by William Collins and Co. Ltd. (London). This quotation is from the Everyman's Library (New York: Knopf, 1991) translated from the Russian by Manya Harari and Max Hayward, p. 332.

PAGE 67   "Man's conquest," George St. George, *Siberia—The New Frontier* (New York, D. McKay Co., 1969), p. 450, cited in Josh Newell and Emma Wilson, *The Russian Far East: Forests, Biodiversity Hotspots, and Industrial Developments* (Tokyo: Friends of the Earth—Japan, 1996), p. 11.

PAGE 68   Simon Schama, *Landscape and Memory* (Toronto: Vintage Canada, 1995), p. 73.

PAGE 69–70   Quotes from Andrei Laletin are from an interview with the author.

PAGE 75   Andrew Wiget and Olga Balalaeva, "Will Drilling Transform Western Siberia, Sakhalin into 'National Sacrifice Areas'?", Pacific Environment and Resources Centre bulletin, June 1997.

PAGE 76   Quoted in Andrew Meier, "Cursed Cornucopia," *Time*, December 29, 1997.

PAGES 79–80   Quotes from Anatoly Lebeder are from an interview with the author.

PAGE 85   Quotes from Dimitri Ahsenov are from an interview with the author.

PAGES 86–87   Quotes from Stewart Cohen and Glenn Juday are from interviews with the author.

PAGE 88   Dr. Russell A. Mittermeier, president of the Washington, DC-based Conservation International, quoted in "Soviet 'Amazon' in Jeopardy," Green Leaf Weekly, September 9, 1991.

PAGE 88   Quoted in Andrew Meier, "Cursed Cornucopia," *Time*, December 29, 1997.

CHAPTER 7

PAGE 89   Fridtjof Nansen, "Farewell to Norway," *Farthest North* (London: George Newnes, Ltd., 1898), pp. 88–89.

PAGES 90–91   All quotes from Knut-Erik Helle are from an interview with the author.

PAGE 91   "Small and isolated," "The Boreal Forest: A Brief Status Report," background paper to the 4th Taiga Rescue Network conference, Tartu, Estonia, October 6–8, 1998.

PAGE 93   Karin Lindahl, *Forestry in the Boreal Region—Toward Sustainability*, in press. Emphasis is mine.

PAGE 93 "The Scandinavian Forestry Model," Taiga Rescue Network Fact Sheet, May 1997.

PAGE 93–94 Species extinction, "Old-Growth Taiga Forest—A Challenge to Nature Protection," published by the Nature Protection Unit of Finland's Forest and Park Service, 1996.

PAGE 95 Forest depletion, "Extinction Wave Threatens Species of Old-Growth Forests," *Kainuun Sanomat* (regional newspaper), February 6, 1998.

PAGE 95 Quotes from Kaisa Raitio are from an interview with the author.

PAGE 96 FSC Notes, *Forest Stewardship Council Newsletter* 8 (July/ August 1998).

PAGES 96–97 Assessed sites, Karin Lindahl, "Sweden—An Importer of Wood Fibre and Exporter of Wood Products," in *Swedish Forestry Goes East: A Report on the Swedish Forest Industry's Involvement in the Russian Forest Sector,* by Karin Lindahl, Alexei Grigoriev, and Dimitri Aksenov (Stockholm, Swedish Society for Nature Conservation, 1997).

PAGE 97 Quotes from Jan Henricksson are from an interview with the author.

PAGE 99 "Logging in Sweden," *Taiga News* 26 (January 1999).

PAGE 100 Quotes from Jonas Rudberg are from an interview with the author.

PAGES 101–102 Ulf Osterblom, "The Role of the Forest Owners' Associations in the Development of Privately-Owned Forestry in Sweden," a paper delivered at a conference of the International Union of Forestry Research Organizations, "Private Forestry: Chances and Challenges for Countries in Transition," Krakow, Poland, August 29–September 2, 1994.

PAGE 102 "One-stop shop," interview with the author.

PAGE 103 Paul Mitchell-Banks, "Tenure Arrangements for Facilitating Community Forestry in British Columbia" (Ph.D. diss., University of British Columbia, 1999).

PAGE 108 "Major step," "Pan Asia Paper Company Is Established," Norske Skog press release, February 2, 1999.

PAGE 108 "Norwegian," "The Vanishing Old Growth Forests of Norway," *Taiga News* 24 (April 1998).

PAGES 109–110   For background on the Green Belt and Karelia, I'm indebted to Eva Kleinn for the use of her dissertation, "Planning and Geoecological Assessment for a World Heritage Site Nomination in the 'Green Belt of Fennoscandia'" (Karlsruhe: University of Karlsruhe, 1998) and Otso Ovaskainen for his "Survey of Old-Growth Forests in Northwest Russia" (Finnish Nature League Publications, 1998).

PAGE 110   Eva Kleinn, "Planning and Geoecological Assessment," p. 7

PAGE 111   Quotes from Otso Ovaskainen are from an interview with the author.

PAGE 113   From an untitled article written by Pauli Leontjeff, *Oma Mua* [*Own Country*] Karelian newspaper, May 5, 1997.

PAGE 115   Quote from Virpi Sahi is from an interview with the author.

CHAPTER 8

PAGE 117   "Rate of cutting," "Taking the Axe to Alberta's Forests," *Globe and Mail,* June 22, 1998.

PAGE 118   Ibid.

PAGE 119   Ibid.

PAGE 120   "Pulp Mills in Alberta's Boreal Forest," *Environment News,* September 1989.

PAGE 122   Japan Environmental Exchange questionnaire sent to Japanese companies (Tokyo, April 1995), p. 5, cited in Josh Newell and Emma Wilson, *The Russian Far East: Forests, Biodiversity Hotspots, and Industrial Developments* (Tokyo: Friends of the Earth—Japan, 1996), p. 21.

PAGE 123   Elizabeth May, *At the Cutting Edge: The Crisis in Canada's Forests* (Toronto: Key Porter, 1998), p. 183.

PAGE 125   *Daishowa v. Friends of the Lubicon,* reasons for decision dismissing claim for a permanent injunction, April 13, 1998. Ontario Court of Justice (General Division), Court File No. 95-CQ-59707, between Daishowa Inc. (Plaintiff) and Friends of the Lubicon Kevin Thomas, Ed Bianchi, Stephen Kenda, Jane Doe and Persons Unknown (Defendants), paragraph #69.

PAGE 126   "Would fill a woodlot," quote from Christopher Genovali's April 1988 Boreal Forest Network website report, "New $900 Million Paper Mill by Daishowa Marubeni International Equals More

Destruction for the Lubicon." Available at <www.borealnet.org/oilandpulp/diashowadestroys.html>.

PAGE 127   "The Lubicon cling," ibid.

PAGE 129   Oil and gas exploration, report by biologist Brian Horejsi of Western Wildlife Environments Consulting, cited by Christopher Genovali in "Sinking in the Oil Sands: North America's Largest ($25 Billion) Oil Development Scheme Will Severely Impact Lubicon Traditional Territory," Taiga Rescue Network web news, April 1998.

PAGES 129–130   Ben Parfitt, *Forest Follies: Adventures and Misadventures in the Great Canadian Forest* (Madeira Park, BC: Harbour, 1998), pp. 119–120, 122.

PAGE 130   Ibid.

PAGE 130   Filtering tar sands, "Liquid Gold: Thirty Years in the Alberta Tar sands," supplement to the *Calgary Herald* and *Edmonton Journal*, September 18, 1997.

PAGES 131–132   Increasing reliance on tar sands, "Alberta's Oil Sands Come of Age," *Globe and Mail*, November 29, 1997.

PAGES 131–132   Birds in jeopardy, "Expansion of Oil Sands Is Going Too Far—Report," *Edmonton Journal*, October 14, 1997.

CHAPTER 9

PAGES 135–137   Quotes from Garry Raven and Fabian Morrisseau are from interviews with the author.

PAGE 140   Ben Parfitt, *Forest Follies: Adventures and Misadventures in the Great Canadian Forest* (Madeira Park, BC: Harbour, 1998), p. 128.

PAGE 140   "What's happened," interview with the author.

PAGES 143–144   Quotes from Rodney Northey and Don Sullivan are from an interview with the author.

PAGE 144   "Some species," September 1996 letter regarding Louisiana Pacific's harvesting activities in the Manitoba boreal forest.

PAGE 145   Kristin Laun-Jensen and Burkhard Mausberg, "The Fight to Protect Manitoba Forests," *Toronto Star*, October 29, 1998.

PAGE 146   "Firm Gets Go-Ahead to Log Massive Manitoba Forest," *Globe and Mail*, June 22, 1999.

PAGE 148   From the introduction of the final consolidated report on Lands for Life, October 30, 1998.

PAGES 149–150   Road-free areas, Parfitt, *Forest Follies,* p. 18, 20.

PAGE 150   "Every hectare," Canadian Parks and Wilderness Society, "Loggers Target Ontario Parks for Cutting," *The Wilderness Activist* 1(6) (1998), cited in *Sustainable Development of the Boreal Forest: Interaction of Ecological, Social and Business Feedbacks,* by F. Stuart Chapin and Gail Whiteman, Ecological Society of America, 1998. Published by Conservation Ecology at <www.consecol.org/Journal/vol2/iss2/art12/>.

PAGE 151   Civil disobedience campaigns, "Fight for Northern Ontario Escalating," *Globe and Mail,* August 5, 1998.

PAGE 152   "Ontario Today," CBC interview with Dave Stevens, November 23, 1998. Ontario's environmental commissioner is an independent officer of the legislative assembly. The commissioner monitors the government's compliance with the Environmental Bill of Rights.

PAGE 153   "A Collective Statement of Conservation Concern from the Scientific and Academic Communities Regarding Lands for Life, Ontario, Canada," November 25, 1998. The statement was prepared by a joint conservation science team known as the Partnership for Public Lands, a group that included the World Wildlife Fund Canada, the Federation of Ontario Naturalists, and the Wildlands League, a chapter of the Canadian Parks and Wilderness Society.

CHAPTER 10

PAGE 158   Hugh Brody, *Maps and Dreams* (Vancouver: Douglas & McIntyre, 1981), p. 177.

PAGE 164   *Dene Tha': Traditional Land-Use and Occupancy Study* (Calgary: Arctic Institute of North America, 1997), p. 24. Copyright The Dene Tha' Nation, 1997.

PAGES 165–169   The methodology follows that described in *Mapping How We Use Our Land: Using Participatory Action Research,* by Mike Robinson, Terry Garvin, and Gordon Hodgson (Calgary: Arctic Institute of North America, 1994).

PAGES 167–168   Interviews with Dene elders are from *Traditional Land-Use and Occupancy Study,* pp. 78-85.

PAGE 170   Michael D. Robinson and Karim-Aly S. Kassam, *Sami Potatoes: Living with Reindeer and Perestroika* (Calgary: Bayeux Arts

Inc., 1998), 21.

PAGE 171   "Dedicated to," ibid., pp. 1–3.

PAGE 171   "When you create," interview with the author.

PAGE 171   "Make our work," Robinson and Kassam, *Sami Potatoes*, p. 33.

PAGE 172   "Social and cultural," Raphael Kaplinsky, *The Economies of Small* (London: Intermediate Technology Publications, 1990), cited in *Sami Potatoes*, p. 34.

PAGE 173   *Delgamuukw v. British Columbia* (11 December 1997), 23799 at para. 168, note 3 (S.C.C.).

PAGE 173–175   Monique M. Ross, Michael Robinson, and Cheryl Sharvit, *Resource Developments on Traditional Lands: The Duty to Consult*, abstract paper, 1998, pp. 25-34. The story presented here is an edited version of the original.

PAGE 176   Government involvement in comanagement, ibid.

PAGE 178   The proportion of all Canadian logging in BC is an estimate by the Canadian Council of Forest Ministers, *Compendium of Canadian Forestry Statistics, 1994* (Ottawa: C.C.F.M., 1995). The average annual cut during the 1990s is cited from the BC Ministry of Forests' annual reports from 1991–92 to 1994–95. Both figures quoted from Elizabeth May, *At the Cutting Edge: The Crisis in Canada's Forests* (Toronto: Key Porter, 1998), p. 188.

PAGES 182–183   Quotes from Don Sullivan and James Allen are from interviews with the author.

CHAPTER 11

PAGE 185   Bill Devall, Afterword to *Ecoforestry: The Art and Science of Sustainable Forest Use,* ed. Alan R. Drengson and Duncan M. Taylor (Gabriola Island, BC: New Society Publishers, 1997), p. 276.

PAGE 186   Herb Hammond, *Seeing the Forest Among the Trees: The Case for Wholistic Forest Use* (Vancouver: Polestar, 1991), p. 311.

PAGE 187   "To maintain and," Orville Camp, "Critical Elements of Forest Sustainability," in *Ecoforestry*, p. 35.

PAGE 187   "A community of hundreds," Jerry Mander, Foreword to *Ecoforestry,* p. 12.

PAGE 188   Fire, wind, and decay, Herb Hammond, *The Boreal Forest: Options for Ecologically Responsible Use,* a report prepared for the Yukon Conservation Society, April 1994, p. 32. The following section is paraphrased from this report.

PAGES 190–191   Ibid, p. 34.

PAGE 193   Donald McPhillimy, "A Forest for Scotland," in *Ecoforestry,* p. 161.

PAGE 194   David Whyte's comments are from the lecture "Disappearing Forests Mean Disappearing Cultures," presented at the 4th Taiga Rescue Network conference in Estonia, October 6, 1998.

PAGE 195   Interview with the author.

PAGES 196–197   Quotes from Herald Herlander are from an interview with the author.

PAGE 198   Quotes from Jutta Kill are from an interview with the author.

PAGE 199   Quote from Josh Newell is from an interview with the author.

PAGE 200   "To make the principles," F. Stuart Chapin and Gail Whiteman, *Sustainable Development of the Boreal Forest: Interaction of Ecological, Social and Business Feedbacks,* 1998.

PAGE 200   "If carbon taxes," ibid.

References

The following is a selected bibliography of sources used in writing *Vanishing Halo*. Newspaper articles, secondary sources, and other material are cited, where appropriate, in the endnotes.

Bastedo, Jamie. *Reaching North: A Celebration of the Subarctic.* Red Deer, AB: Red Deer College Press, 1998.

Briffa, K.R., F.H. Schweingruber, P.D. Jones, T.J. Osborn, S.G. Shiyatov, and E.A. Vaganov. "Reduced Sensitivity of Recent Tree-Growth to Temperature at High Northern Latitudes," *Nature* 391 (12 February 1998).

Brody, Hugh. *Maps and Dreams.* Vancouver: Douglas & McIntyre, 1981.

Brownson, J.M. Jamil. *In Cold Margins.* Montana: Northern Rim Press, 1997.

Cannings, Richard, and Sydney Cannings. *Mountains and Northern Forests.* Vancouver: Greystone, 1998.

Chapin, Stuart F., and Gail Whiteman. *Sustainable Development of the Boreal Forest: Interaction of Ecological, Social and Business Feedbacks.* Ecological Society of America, 1998. Published by Conservation Ecology at <www.consecol.org/Journal/vol2/iss2/art12/>.

Chebakova, I.V. *National Parks of Russia: A Guidebook.* Moscow: Biodiversity Conservation Centre, 1997.

Cohen, Stewart J., ed. *Mackenzie Basin Impact Study,* Final Report for Environment Canada, 1997.

Dene Tha' Nation. *Dene Tha': Traditional Land-Use and Occupancy Study.* Calgary: Arctic Institute of Canada, 1997. Copyright The Dene Tha' Nation, 1997.

Drengson, Alan R., and Duncan M. Taylor, eds. *Ecoforestry: The Art and Science of Sustainable Forest Use.* Gabriola Island, BC: New Society Publishers, 1997.

Dudley, Nigel, et al. *Forests and Climate Change.* Report for World Wildlife Federation International, November 1998.

Environment Canada. *Canada Country Study: Climate Impacts and Adaptation,* vol. 3, 1997.

Federal Court of Canada, Trial Division. *Manitoba's Future Forest Alliance and Don Sullivan and the Minister of Environment, the Minister of Fisheries and Oceans, and Tolko Manitoba Inc.* Application Record Volume VIII: Concise memorandum of fact and law for the applicants. Court File no: T-434-98.

Forest Stewardship Council. *FSC Notes* 8 (July/August 1998).

Fuller, William A., and John C. Holmes. *The Life of the Far North: Our Living World of Nature.* New York: McGraw Hill, 1972.

Hammond, Herb. *Seeing the Forest Among the Trees: The Case for Wholistic Forest Use.* Vancouver: Polestar, 1991.

———— *The Boreal Forest: Options for Ecologically Responsible Use.* Prepared for the Yukon Conservation Society, April 1994.

Hollow Water First Nation Native Alcohol and Drug Addiction Program. *Traditional Ways of Healing from Addictions.* Copyright 1998.

Kleinn, Eva. "Planning and Geoecological Assessment for a World Heritage Site Nomination in the 'Green Belt of Fennoscandia.'" Karlsruhe, Germany: University of Karlsruhe graduate paper, May 1998.

Kurz, Werner A., and Michael J. Apps. "Retrospective Assessment of Carbon Flows in Canadian Boreal Forests." In *Forest Ecosystems, Forest Management and the Global Carbon Cycle,* ed. by M.J. Apps and D.T. Price. NATO ASI Series. Heidelberg: Springer-Verlag, 1995.

Kurz, Werner A., et al. "Global Climate Change: Disturbance Regimes and Biospheric Feedbacks of Temperate and Boreal Forests." In *Biotic Feedbacks in the Global Climatic System: Will the Warming Feed the Warming?* ed. by George M. Woodwell, and Fred T. Mackenzie. New York, Oxford: Oxford University Press, 1995.

Kurz, Werner A., Sarah J. Beukema, and Michael J. Apps. "Carbon Budget Implications of the Transition from Natural to Managed Disturbance Regimes in Forest Landscapes." In *Mitigation and Adaptation Strategies for Global Change*. Belgium: Kluwer Academic Publishers, 1998.

Last, John, Konia Trouton, and David Pengelly. *Taking Our Breath Away: The Health Effects of Air Pollution and Climate Change*. Vancouver: David Suzuki Foundation, 1998.

Leopold, Aldo. *A Sand County Almanac*. New York: Oxford University Press, 1966.

Lindahl, Karin, Alexei Grigoriev, and Dimitri Aksenov. *Swedish Forest Industry Goes East: A Report on the Swedish Forest Industry's Involvement in the Russian Forest Sector*. Stockholm: Swedish Society for Nature Conservation, 1997.

May, Elizabeth. *At the Cutting Edge: The Crisis in Canada's Forests*. Toronto: Key Porter, 1998.

Newell, Josh, and Emma Wilson. *The Russian Far East: Forests, Biodiversity Hotspots, and Industrial Developments*. Tokyo: Friends of the Earth–Japan, 1996.

Ovaskainen, Otso. *Survey of Old-Growth Forests in Northwest Russia*. Helsinki: Finnish Nature League Publications, 1998.

Pan-European Biodiversity Conservation for Children and Ministers: Vision from the East. Moscow: Biodiversity Conservation Center, 1998.

Parfitt, Ben. *Forest Follies: Adventures and Misadventures in the Great Canadian Forest*. Madeira Park, BC: Harbour, 1998.

Perry, David A. *Forest Ecosystems*. Baltimore: John Hopkins University Press, 1994.

Price, D.T., D.H. Halliwell, M.J. Apps, W.A. Kurz, and S.R. Curry. "Comprehensive Assessment of Carbon Stocks and Fluxes in a Boreal-Cordilleran Forest Management Unit." Natural Resources Canada abstract, 1997.

Proceedings for a Circumpolar Conference on Aboriginal People and Comanagement Practice (November 20–24, 1995). Arctic Institute of North America, 1996.

Pruitt, William O., Jr. *Boreal Ecology*. London: Edward Arnold Publishers, 1978.

———— *Wild Harmony: The Cycle of Life in the Northern Forest.* Saskatoon, SK: Western Producer Prairie Books, 1983.

Robinson, M.P., and M.M. Ross "Traditional Land Use and Occupancy Studies and Their Impact on Forest Planning and Management in Alberta." *Forestry Chronicle* 73 (5) (September/October 1997).

Robinson, Michael, and Elmer Ghostkeeper. "Native and Local Economics: A Consideration of Economic Evolution and the Next Economy." *Arctic* (Journal of the Arctic Institute of North America) 40 (2) (June 1987).

Robinson, Michael D., and Karim-Aly S. Kassam. *Sami Potatoes: Living with Reindeer and Perestroika.* Calgary: Bayeux Arts Inc., 1998.

Robinson, Mike, Terry Garvin, and Gordon Hodgson. *Mapping How We Use Our Land: Using Participatory Action Research.* Calgary: Arctic Institute of North America, 1994.

Romm, Joseph J., and Charles B. Curtis. "Mideast Oil Forever?" *Atlantic Monthly* (April 1996).

Ross, Monique M., Michael Robinson, and Cheryl Sharvit. *Resource Developments on Traditional Lands: The Duty to Consult.* Abstract paper, 1998.

Schama, Simon. *Landscape and Memory.* Toronto: Vintage Canada, 1996.

Senate of Canada. *Proceedings of the Standing Senate Committee on Agriculture and Forestry: Subcommittee on Boreal Forest,* the Honourable Doris Anderson, Chair. Issues I, II, and III, March 13, March 20, and April 7, 1997.

Suzuki, David, with Amanda McConnell. *The Sacred Balance: Rediscovering Our Place in Nature.* Vancouver: Greystone, 1997.

Wein, Ross W., Roderick R. Riewe, and Ian R. Methven, eds. *Resources and Dynamics of the Boreal Zone.* Ottawa: Association of Canadian Universities for Northern Studies, 1983.

The following is a selection of websites consulted for *Vanishing Halo*:

North American Lichen Project, Conservation Ecology and Sustainable Development of the Boreal Forest, Environment Canada's Boreal Forest page, Central and Western Siberia Boreal and Taiga Forests, An Introduction to the Sami People, Welcome to the BOREAS Project,

MacKenzie Basin Impact Study, Northern Forestry Centre, FFI Frontier News, WWF Living Planet, The Carbon Bomb: Climate Change and the Fate of the Northern Boreal Forest, Finnish Nature League, Climate Change Network, Northern Alaska Environmental Centre, Canadian Model Forest Network, Wildwoods, Save Our Snowforest Campaign, Lands for Life, Gordon Bonan's home page, Stockholm Environment Institute, European Forest Institute, *Earth Times* Online News, Biodiversity in the Boreal Shield Ecozone, Canadian Parks and Wilderness Society, Alaskan Boreal Forest Council, Russian Far East, United Nations Environment Program, Global Climate Change, Silva Forest Foundation, Northern Rim Press, Taiga Rescue Network.

Index

The David Suzuki Foundation:
Working Together for a Sustainable Future

The David Suzuki Foundation was established to work for a world of hope in which our species thrives in balance with the productive capacity of the Earth.

Our mission is to find solutions to the root causes of our most threatening environmental problems. Then, we work with our supporters and their communities to implement those solutions for a sustainable future.

Our mandate is broad, ranging from projects on climate change, air, soil, water, fisheries, forestry, energy, and liveable cities, to defining the foundations of sustainability, how social change occurs, and the potential of new economic models.

We can only accomplish this with the support of concerned citizens who care about the environment. We invite you to help.

JOIN OUR PARTNERSHIP ... JOIN THE FOUNDATION!

To find out how you can become a Friend of the Foundation, or to make a donation, contact:

THE DAVID SUZUKI FOUNDATION
219-2211 WEST FOURTH AVENUE
VANCOUVER, BC, CANADA V6K 4S2
PHONE (604) 732-4228; FAX (604) 732-0752

Thank you very much for your support!